KT-197-657

Berlitz

Vienna

Text by: Jack Altman
Principal Photographer: Glyn Genin
Updated by: Beryl Dhanjal
Edited by: Jane Hutchings
Series Editor: Tony Halliday

Berlitz® POCKET GUIDE

Vienna

Eighth Edition 2004

PHOTOGRAPHY
Austrian Tourist Board 40 (H.Wiesenhofer), 75 (Bohnacker), 76 (Herzberger), 81 (Berger), 82 (Kalmar), 93 (Bartl); Jack Altman 94; Berlitz 78; Beryl Dhanjal 62; Jon Davidson 54, 84; Glyn Genin 6, 12, 114, 15, 19, 22, 24, 26, 28, 31, 32, 34, 36, 37, 38, 46, 49, 52, 55, 57, 59, 63, 64, 65, 66, 68, 69, 87, 88, 89, 91, 95, 96; Maria Lord 33, 48, 51, 62; Mark Read 70, 72; Museum D. Stadt Wien 17; Vienna Tourist Board 9, 43, 44.
Cover picture: Jon Davidson

CONTACTING THE EDITORS
Every effort has been made to provide accurate information in this publication, but changes are inevitable. The publisher cannot be responsible for any resulting loss, inconvenience or injury. We would appreciate it if readers would call our attention to any errors or outdated information by contacting Berlitz Publishing, PO Box 7910, London SE1 1WE, England. Fax: (44) 20 7403 0290;
e-mail: berlitz@apaguide.co.uk
www.berlitzpublishing.com

Schönbrunn, Empress Maria Theresa's opulent rococo palace and gardens
(page 64)

The Secession Building, housing Gustav Klimt's 34-m (112-ft) long *Beethoven Frieze* (page 52)

Stephansdom, the cathedral, at the heart of Vienna's Innere Stadt (page 25)

TOP TEN ATTRACTIONS

Quirky decoration and undulating façades at the Kunsthaus Wien (page 58)

A spectacular performance by the Lipizzaner stallions at the Spanish Riding School (page 42)

The Museum of Modern Art, Architecture Centre, kids' Zoom and multimedia exhibitions can all be found in the MuseumsQuartier (page 51)

Karlsplatz has numerous attractions in addition to the Karlskirche (page 54)

Raphael at the Kunsthistorisches Museum (page 49)

Klimt's *The Kiss* among the treasures at the Belvedere (page 58)

The magnificent Hofburg, the imperial palace of the Habsburgs (page 40)

CONTENTS

Fact Sheets

INTRODUCTION

The elegant Viennese have what is known as *Wiener Lebens-art*, a cultured appreciation of all the pleasures of life. This is reflected not only in Vienna's glorious art, music and architecture, theatres and coffee houses, and its passion for glittering balls, but where else would you find vineyards within the city's limits? In 2001, the Innere Stadt (Old City) was designated a UNESCO World Heritage Site, a well-deserved honour for an area that embraces baroque palaces, elegant shops, the famous Burgtheater and Staatsoper (Opera House), and a maze of narrow medieval streets winding around the cathedral of Stephansdom. The Innere Stadt isn't the only UNESCO World Heritage Site in Vienna: Schloss Schönbrunn joined the list in 1996.

Yet Vienna, with a population of 1.5 million, isn't preserved as a museum exhibit. Old places are revamped and given new uses, and various recent constructions, from the whimsy of Hundertwasser's garbage incinerator to the skyscraping Millennium Tower, add a 21st-century dimension. In the historic centre, projects such as the MuseumsQuartier blend old and new to enhance the cityscape.

> **Vienna is divided into 23 districts. The First District, the historic Innere Stadt (Old City), was declared a UNESCO World Heritage Site in 2001.**

A further factor in UNESCO's recognition is that since the 16th century, Vienna has been universally acknowledged as the musical capital of Europe. And the music goes on: you can still hear the waltzes of Johann Strauss – only he could describe the muddy brown Danube as blue. At the Opera House, imagine yourself to be Mozart's Don Giovanni, or one of his beautiful conquests, and then go off to a *Heuriger* wine-garden on the edge of the Vienna Woods for a late-night glass of white wine and a gloriously sentimental song. Or enjoy the beer and something electronic in the Bermuda Triangle, the city's clubbing district.

Vienna is a town with space to relax, and its rural setting induces a more easygoing attitude to life than that found in other modern cities of comparable size.

Tradition and Modernity

The Viennese are proud of their city's heritage and achieve both continuity and change: they have renovated the grand old hotels and coffee houses, and the clientele – the artists, writers, thinkers and dreamers – have now been joined by TV producers, advertising people and tourists. Viennese fashion designers have taken the time-honoured warm woollen *Loden* fabric – still a great defence against the winter winds – and given it a more innovative cut and brighter colours than the traditional olive green jackets and overcoats. The revered Burgtheater is

---

The Waltz

Music in Vienna is fuelled not only by its hallowed classical tradition, but also by the joy of its waltzes. The waltz began as a heavy, plodding triple-time German dance known as a *Ländler*, which the Viennese transformed into a whirling moment of fairyland. The man who brought the waltz to popular dance halls in 1819 was Joseph Lanner, leader of a small band. He took on a young viola player named Johann Strauss and the waltz took off in a big way. The group grew to become an orchestra and Strauss broke away to form his own – Lanner sadly celebrating the occasion with his *Trennungswalzer (Separation Waltz)*. The two conducted a prolonged 'waltz war' for public favour in the cafés of the Prater. The rivalry ended amicably and Strauss played waltzes – *adagio* – at Lanner's funeral.

The glamorous Opernball, highlight of Vienna's ball season

constantly upsetting its older public with revolutionary productions by uncomfortable authors such as Thomas Bernhardt.

The grandeur of the Habsburg Empire's royal collections include European masterpieces to enjoy, but Vienna also displays its 20th-century masters – Klimt, Schiele and Kokoschka – who shocked the public of their day.

Vienna offers an astonishing choice of museums, from the sublime to the surprising, from art and high culture to *schnapps* and re-usable coffins (many of these can be visited for free or at reduced rates with the Vienna Card, available from the tourist information office). But some things (thankfully) don't change: *Fiakers* (carriages) still drive tourists around the centre; the pure white Lipizzaner stallions dance at the Spanish Riding School; the Café Konditorei still presents a delicious array of gateaux, topped by *Sachertorte*, served with coffee; and the ball season remains the focal point of the social calendar. In January and February, the

The Viennese seldom miss an opportunity for making a flattering remark: 'I kiss your hand, Madam' or 'I am honoured'. Even the familiar greeting *Servus* ('hi' or 'bye') is the latin for 'your servant'.

Opernball at the Opera House and the Philharmoniker Ball at the Musikverein vie with one another as *the* place to see and be seen. Confectioners throw the Zuckerbäckerball and the Kaffeesiederball honours coffee. Doctors, lawyers, even the *Fiaker* cab drivers have their night. Then in May it's the turn of the international celebrities who descend on the city to dance the night away at the Life Ball, an AIDS charity event.

Not Too *Gemütlich*

Vienna's historic role as a crossroads of Eastern and Western European civilisation has taken on a new significance since the collapse of the Soviet bloc and Austria's entry into the European Union in 1995. The city's relaxed atmosphere often comes as a surprise to visitors. The Viennese still seem to have time for the courtesies of the old days. Although recent social innovations have been generally popular in Vienna, the people remain profoundly conservative in their values. Politically the Viennese have always been impossible to define. They cheered their Habsburg emperors and then Napoleon. They welcomed the republican experiment after World War I and then hailed Hitler.

And then they found democracy rather nice, too. It seemed conducive to their legendary taste for *Gemütlichkeit*. Roughly translated, *gemütlich* means comfy and cosy, the quality that takes the rough edges off life. It is part of the famous Viennese charm, a charm also sharpened by undertones of sometimes malicious irony known as *Wiener Schmäh* (Viennese sarcasm). This is much cultivated by the younger generations who know that to thrive in the new century, Vienna must never get too comfy and cosy.

As capital of the Habsburg Empire, Vienna was home not only to Slavs and Hungarians, but also to Germans, and other Europeans. The Jews, too, such a vital force in pre-1938 Vienna, left their mark on the culture: psychoanalyst Sigmund Freud, composer Gustav Mahler and playwright Arthur Schnitzler among others. Modern Vienna recognises their suffering in the Nazi era. Now, new generations of Poles, Italians, Turks, Croats and other ethnic groups from the former Yugoslavia, as well as from outside Europe, have again swollen the workforce. There is a sizable group of prosperous, and so more leisurely, Russians. The language is, of course, German, but, like Viennese cuisine, it has that distinctive Viennese way of incorporating elements from the many ethnic groups that make up the city's population.

Vienna, with the Karlskirche

A BRIEF HISTORY

From earliest times, Vienna was a crossroads for people migrating between eastern and western Europe. The first identifiable inhabitants of the area were Illyrians who sailed up the Danube from the Balkan peninsula. Celts migrating from Gaul around 500BC founded the town of Vindobona ('Shining Field'), which the Romans took over in the 1st century AD.

Romans and Barbarians

Sent from Britain to defend the empire's eastern European frontier, Rome's soldiers built their garrison in what is today the Inner City's Hoher Markt. They had their work cut out fending off invasions of the Teutons and Slavs. Emperor Marcus Aurelius personally led the fight against the barbarians, but died in Vindobona of the plague in AD180. A hundred years later, another Roman emperor, Probus, won the gratitude of subsequent generations by developing vineyards on the slopes of the Wienerwald (Vienna Woods). Today,

Barbarian invader

Probusgasse, a street in the heart of the *Heuriger* wine district of Heiligenstadt, honours his initiative.

Christianity arrived in the 4th century, but was powerless against successive waves of barbarian warriors. Attila the Hun advanced on Vienna in 453, but died before implementing plans for its conquest. The Huns were followed over the next

600 years by Goths, Franks, Avars, Slavs and Magyars, all burning and pillaging their way through the city, even in the face of Charlemagne's pacification efforts at the end of the 8th century. The Frankish king did at least strengthen the hand of the Christians. They had built their first church, Ruprechts-kirche, in 740, and were now able to add two others, Maria am Gestade and Peterskirche.

Babenberg Rule

Stability came in 1156 when the Babenbergs, Bavarian lords who had succeeded a century and a half earlier in driving out the Magyars, were granted the hereditary duchy of Austria by the Holy Roman Emperor.

The first duke, Heinrich II Jasomirgott, set up his court around what is today the Platz am Hof, giving Vienna its first golden era. Art, trade and handicrafts thrived, attracting immigrant German merchants and artisans. Vienna became an important stopover for crusaders. Scottish and Irish monks on their way to Jerusalem founded the monastery of Schottenstift. Babenberg rule brought many new churches, notably the first Stephansdom, as well as several monasteries, elegant residences for the nobility along the broad new thoroughfares, and a fortress on the site of the future Hofburg castle. In 1200, financed with English ransom money paid to liberate King Richard the Lion Heart, a ring of fortifications was built around the Innere Stadt, along what is now the Ringstrasse. It was also the great era of the minstrels and the start of Vienna's long musical tradition.

> **The last Babenburg ruler was Friedrich II (1210–46), known as Friedrich der Streitbare (the Belligerent). He disturbed Vienna's hard-earned peace by picking fights with his barons, seducing the burghers' wives and going off to war at the slightest provocation.**

The Habsburgs

Rudolf der Stifter (the Founder)

In 1246 the male line of the Babenbergs died out and the country fell to Ottokar II of Bohemia. Ottokar was popular with the Viennese. He made attractive additions to the Stephansdom and started on the Hofburg. The people did not appreciate the efforts of the new German king, Rudolf von Habsburg, to gain control of the city. They supported Ottokar, but in 1278 Rudolf triumphed.

Vienna's history for centuries thereafter was a constant confrontation between the Habsburgs' visions of grandeur and world conquest and the citizens' taste for the quiet life. Whenever the Habsburgs went about their empire-building, under Maximilian I, Karl V and Ferdinand I, Vienna was painfully neglected.

The most popular rulers were the ones who preferred to stay at home and build things. Rudolf der Stifter (the Founder) created the university in 1365 and turned the Romanesque Stephansdom into the Gothic structure you see today. Friedrich III completed the work and won Rome's approval for Vienna to become a bishopric in 1469. The Viennese showed their appreciation by burying him in the cathedral. As his tomb attests, it was Friedrich who dreamed up the grandiose motto: AEIOU, *'Austria Est Imperare Orbi Universo'*, for which an English approximation might be 'Austria's Empire Is Our Universe'.

The 15th century was not all sweetness and light: in 1421, more than 200 Jews were burned alive in their quarter around Judenplatz and the remainder were driven out of the city. The Hungarian king Matthias Corvinus occupied Vienna from 1485 to 1490. He's remembered for his remark: 'Let others wage war while you, happy Austria, arrange marriages. What Mars gives to others, you receive from Venus.' The reference was to the Habsburgs' knack of expanding their empire through judicious mating of their innumerable archdukes and archduchesses, a policy that was used to great advantage by Maximilian I (1493–1519).

Picking up where the Goths and the Magyars left off, the Turks under Suleiman the Magnificent staged a crippling 18-day siege of Vienna in 1529. The suburbs were devastated, but the Innere Stadt held fast and the infidels were finally forced to retreat.

The Habsburg emblem adorns the Hofburg

In the Reformation of the 16th century and the Thirty Years War that followed, the city emerged as a bulwark of the Catholic Church. Having withstood the Muslim Turks, Vienna banned Protestant worship in 1577, and repelled an attack by the Protestant Swedes of Gustav Adolph in 1645.

Jews were allowed back into town, having been confined during the 1620s to a ghetto on the riverside marshlands of Leopoldstadt. Emperor Leopold I was the one to usher Vienna into its glorious baroque era, a feast of architecture and music that scarcely paused to deal with the vicious plague of 1679 and another Turkish siege in 1683. The great soldier and scholar, Prince Eugene of Savoy *(see below)*, was rewarded for his victory over the Turks with ample funds to build the magnificent and now renowned Belvedere Palace. The Auerspergs, Schwarzenbergs and Liechtensteins followed suit with palaces on a more modest, but equally elegant scale.

Karl VI, pretender to the Spanish throne, returned to Vienna more Spanish than Austrian, bringing with him the strict formality and piety of the Spanish court. His renovation of the 12th-century Abbey Klosterneuburg in baroque style was an attempt to create an Austrian version of El Escorial. Similarly, the huge Karlskirche was originally intended to emulate St Peter's in Rome. Vying with Versailles, the Hofburg palace underwent a magnificent expansion which included the building of the Spanish Riding School and the Imperial Library.

Prince Eugene of Savoy (1663–1736)

Sceptical by nature, the Viennese have few authentic heroes; ironically, the greatest was a Frenchman who became the supreme Austrian patriot. A unique blend of military courage, culture and human warmth, Prince Eugene of Savoy was born in Paris in 1663. Unsuccessful in establishing a military career in his own country under Louis XIV, the prince spent a period in a monastery and then went to Austria to seek his fortune. He arrived in Vienna in 1683, just in time to help out with the campaigns against the Turks. Over the next 30 years he fought brilliantly for Austria against the Turks and the French, rising to the position of commander-in-chief in 1697. Small of stature and always dressed in a rough brown uniform, simple as a monk's, he was known to his soldiers as 'the little Capuchin'.

Maria Theresa and Napoleon

After this feverish construction that crowned the empire-building efforts of the male Habsburgs, the Viennese were delighted to be able to relax under the maternal eye of Maria Theresa (1740–80). Pious, warm and sentimental, this mother of 16 children had an unerring feel for the moods of her capital's citizens. She was an enthusiastic patron of the arts, especially music.

Empress Maria Theresa

She loved to have concerts and operas performed at her newly completed Schönbrunn Palace, which she infinitely preferred to the more austere Hofburg. Her orchestra director was Christoph Gluck. Young Joseph Haydn sang in the Vienna Boys' Choir, and six-year-old Wolfgang Amadeus Mozart won Maria Theresa's heart by asking for the hand of one of her daughters. (In the event, the daughter in question, Marie-Antoinette, was destined to lose her head for somebody else.) In the following years, these three composers – Gluck, Haydn and Mozart – launched Vienna's reputation as a city of music.

Maria Theresa lulled the Viennese into a false sense of security. Her son Joseph II (1780–90), very serious-minded and not particularly tactful, shocked them into a reluctant awareness of the revolutionary times that were coming. He rushed through a series of far-reaching reforms, making life easier for peasants, Protestants and Jews. But the conservative Viennese were not ready. They were startled to see him open up the city by tearing down the wall around the Innere Stadt, and were impressed by the bureaucratic machine he installed to run the empire.

People felt more secure with the cynical and not at all reform-minded Franz II, particularly following the news from France of the execution of Joseph's sister Marie-Antoinette. On seeing the strange tricolour flag hoisted by the new envoy of the French republic, the Viennese promptly tore it to shreds – along with diplomatic relations between Austria and France. They were less bumptious when Napoleon's armies arrived in November 1805 and the French emperor moved into Maria Theresa's beloved Schönbrunn on his way to further glories at Austerlitz.

Once more, the Habsburgs' secret weapon in foreign policy, politically astute marriages, came into play. Now, faced in 1810 with saving what was left of the empire, Emperor Franz did not hesitate to give his daughter Marie-Louise in marriage to his enemy Napoleon. The Viennese did not protest – anything for a quiet life.

The Long 19th Century

The Napoleonic era ended with one of the city's most splendid moments, the Congress of Vienna in 1815, organised by Franz's crafty chancellor Metternich for the postwar carving up of Napoleon's Europe. Franz was happy to leave the diplomatic shenanigans to Metternich while he supervised a non-stop spectacle of banquets, balls and concerts – all the things the Viennese loved best. Many considered Franz more successful than Metternich. 'This Congress does not make progress,' said Belgium's Prince de Ligne, 'it dances.'

For the next 30 years or so the city relaxed for a quiet period of gracious living, an almost democratic time, with the Prater park a favourite outing for royalty and workers alike. And it was time for more music. Beethoven had

Johann Strauss gets the Viennese waltzing

become the darling of an aristocracy eager to make amends for its shameful neglect of Mozart. But in general the taste was more for the waltzes of Johann Strauss, both father and son.

In 1848 Vienna became caught up in a wave of revolution that spread across Europe in support of national independence and political reform. Ferdinand, the most sweet-natured but also the most dim-witted of Habsburg emperors, exclaimed when he heard that disgruntled citizens were marching on his Hofburg, 'Are they allowed to do that?' He fled town before getting an answer. Metternich was forced out of power, and the mob hanged the war minister Theodor Latour from a lamppost before imperial troops brutally re-established order.

Ferdinand abdicated and his deadly earnest nephew, Franz Joseph, took over. Grimly aware of his enormous burden, Franz Joseph concentrated throughout his 68-year reign on defending his family's interests and preserving as much of

Empress Elisabeth (Sissy)

the empire as possible. Vienna offered him a paradoxically triumphant arena in which to preside over inevitable imperial decline. Prospering from the industrial revolution, the city enthusiastically developed the Ringstrasse, with imposing residences for capitalism's new aristocracy and expanded residential districts for the burgeoning bourgeoisie.

The World Fair in 1873 sang the city's praises and people travelled from Europe and America to see the new opera house, concert halls and theatres. The Austrian Empire's cultural achievements were consecrated in monumental form before the empire itself disappeared. Brahms, Bruckner, Mahler, Lehar and Strauss provided the music. At the Secession Gallery, a group of young artists introduced a new style of art, which came to be known as *Jugendstil* (Art Nouveau; *see page 53*). Only a spoilsport like Sigmund Freud over at the university would suggest that the Viennese examine the depths of their unconscious for the seeds of their darker impulses. They, of course, paid no attention. As the intellectuals in the coffee houses clucked disapprovingly, the town waltzed on. A would-be painter named Adolf Hitler left town in disgust at this lack of seriousness, blaming the Jews and Slavs he had encountered in Vienna for the problems of the 'true Germans'.

The End of the Empire

Having lost his son Rudolf through a suicide in Mayerling, and his wife Elisabeth to an assassin's knife in Geneva, Franz Joseph was stricken but fatalistic when he heard that his heir, Archduke Franz Ferdinand, had been shot in Sarajevo. The world war (1914–18) that followed ended the Habsburg Empire and left Vienna in economic and social ruin. Vienna lost its hinterland of Czechoslovakia, Hungary, parts of Poland, Romania and what was then Yugoslavia, all of which had brought it economic prosperity and cultural enrichment.

While the state opera could boast Richard Strauss as its director, and the old creative spirit re-emerged in architecturally progressive public housing, things were not the same. The city suffered from crippling inflation. Politically polarised, street fighting broke out between Communists and fascist supporters of the government of Engelbert Dollfuss.

In 1934 Dollfuss was assassinated by the outlawed Austrian Nazis in the chancellery on Ballhausplatz. His successor, Kurt von Schuschnigg, succeeded in crushing the *putsch*, but was forced four years later to yield to Hitler's *Anschluss* (German annexation) of Austria – an idea that originally had the support of both left and right.

On 13 March 1938, Hitler's triumphant drive along the Mariahilferstrasse was cheered by the Viennese who saw him as their saviour from the chaos of recent years. He proved the opposite for the city's 180,000 Jews. The brutality of the Austrian Nazis and the spite of many local citizens shocked even those who had witnessed their counterparts at work in Germany. The extermination

> **Hitler's residence in the city is not commemorated. It is recorded that he stayed in a hostel in Meldemannstrasse and that he had a flat at Stumpergasse 31. But there isn't anything to see at either site.**

of the Jews left a great stain on the city and a gaping hole in its cosmopolitan culture.

In some small measure, the city's spirit survived in World War II. Joseph Bürckel, the Nazi Gauleiter overseeing Vienna, warned Goebbels that it was perhaps better to allow satirical cabaret to continue: 'One must give more scope to Viennese humour than is usual in the rest of the Reich.' All humour had evaporated before the bombardments of 1945. The cherished Stephansdom, however, was principally the victim of shelling by SS commandos, who then fled with all the fire-fighting equipment. After the war, Vienna, like Berlin, was divided into four sectors, with the Innere Stadt under the joint administration of the Americans, Russians, British and French. The penury was countered by stoic good humour and a vicious black market.

Austria's neutrality, granted in 1955, made Vienna an appropriate host for the International Atomic Energy Agency, the United Nations Industrial Development Organisation and OPEC (Organisation of Petroleum Exporting Countries). With the status of a world states-man, Chancellor Bruno Kreisky even gave the city a familiar old whiff of international power-brokering.

Modern Vienna's UNO-City

Austria joined the European Union in 1995, once more giving Vienna an active role in Europe. With the entry of an extreme-right party into the government coalition of 2000, the old capital needed all its diplomatic talents to deal with the adverse reaction of its European and American allies.

Historical Landmarks

500BC Celts build town of Vindobona.

1st century AD Romans establish garrison.

4th–9th century Barbarian invasions.

740 Ruprechtskirche is built, the earliest known Christian church.

1156–1246 Babenbergs reign as dukes of Vienna; the first Stephansdom cathedral and precursor of the Hofburg castle is built.

1278 Rudolf von Habsburg launches 640-year dynasty.

1365 University of Vienna founded.

1421 Jewish pogrom; 200 burned to death.

1529 First Turkish siege repelled.

1577 Catholic Church bans Reformation Protestants.

17th century Jews return to found Leopoldstadt ghetto.

1683 Second Turkish siege conquered.

1740–80 Popular Maria Theresa makes her home in Schönbrunn Palace; Haydn and Mozart make Vienna the musical capital.

1780–90 Joseph II's reforms prove unpopular with the Viennese.

1805 Napoleon arrives in Vienna.

1815 The Congress of Vienna carves up Europe while princes dance.

1848 Short-lived revolt drives Metternich from Vienna. Emperor Ferdinand replaced by Franz Joseph (1848–1916).

1873 World Fair celebrates Vienna's grandeur.

1900 Sigmund Freud writes *The Interpretation of Dreams*.

1914–18 Defeat in World War I ends Austrian Empire.

1934 Austrian Nazis assassinate Chancellor Dollfuss.

1938 German annexation *(Anschluss)* of Austria.

1939–45 World War II: Allied bombs devastate city.

1955 Austria granted neutrality.

1995 Austria enters European Union.

1999 Far right Freedom Party election to government causes consternation in Europe and US. Defeated in 2002 elections.

2001 Vienna's Innere Stadt designated a UNESCO World Heritage Site.

2002 The Danube floods part of the city.

WHERE TO GO

GETTING AROUND

Nearly all Vienna's major attractions are packed inside the Innere Stadt (Inner City). This means that places such as the Stephansdom (St Stephen's Cathedral), the Hofburg (Imperial Palace), the Burgtheater (National Theatre), Mozart's house, the Staatsoper (State Opera) and the shops on and around Kärntnerstrasse and the Graben are all within walking distance. Even the Kunsthistorisches Museum (Museum of Fine Arts) and Karlskirche are only just outside the Ringstrasse that marks the medieval precincts of the 1st District.

The best way to view the formidable monuments along the Ringstrasse is by **tram** *(Strassenbahn)*. Trams also cover some 35 routes to outlying districts and provide a good, cheap way of reaching other parts of the city on your trip, for instance Schönbrunn Palace or a *Heuriger* wine garden. The **U-Bahn** subway system has five lines, numbered U1 to U6 (U5 has not yet been built). U1 and U3 intersect in the city centre at Stephansplatz. The other most conveniently located station is Karlsplatz.

Feeling romantic, or just plain footsore, you may take a *Fiaker*, the typical horse-drawn carriage, found at a number of spots around the Innere Stadt, including Stephansplatz, Albertinaplatz and Heldenplatz.

INNERE STADT

Stephansdom

The imposing **Stephansdom** (St Stephen's Cathedral), located right in the heart of Vienna, is the best place to start a city tour.

Left: Maria-Theresien-Platz and the Kunsthistorisches Museum

Whichever way you choose to walk through the Innere Stadt you seem to end up inevitably at the cathedral. For more than eight centuries it has watched over Vienna, weathering city fires, Turkish cannonballs and German and Russian shells.

The steeple, affectionately known as *Steffl* (Stevie), is 137m (449ft) high. Count 343 steps to the **observation platform** at the top, where the view extends northeast to the Czech Republic and southwest to the Semmering Alps.

The main portal takes its name, **Riesentor** (Giant's Gate), from a huge bone found during construction in the 13th century, which was thought to be the shin of a giant drowned in Noah's flood. The bone hung on the door until the Age of Enlightenment, when scientists concluded it was the tibia of a mammoth.

With its Romanesque western façade, Gothic tower and baroque altars, the cathedral epitomises Vienna's grand old

Stephansdom and the Haas Haus

genius for harmonious compromise, here managing to seamlessly meld the austerity, dignity and exuberance of three architectural styles. The Romanesque origins (1240) are strkingly visible in the breathtaking **Heidentürme** (Heathen Towers) and statuary depicting, among others, a griffin and Samson fighting a lion. Above the entrance are Jesus, the Apostles and a veritable menagerie of dragons, lions, reptiles and birds representing evil spirits to be exorcised by the sanctity of the church.

Painted on the wall just inside the main entrance of Stephansdom are the characters 05. This is the secret code of an Austrian resistance movement against the Nazis which began in 1944. The 5 stands for the fifth letter of the alphabet, E, and OE (Ö) is the first sound of Österreich (Austria).

The mainly Gothic structure we see today was built in the 14th and 15th centuries. To support their petition to have Vienna made a bishopric, the Habsburgs hoped to impress the Pope by adding a second tower. But the city fathers preferred to spend the money on strengthening city fortifications against the Turks and Protestants. The north tower was never properly completed, just topped off in 1578 with a nicely frivolous Renaissance cupola. Part of the Stephansdom's charm derives from the asymmetry of its steeple, set to one side.

From atop the North Tower (accessible by lift), you have a fine view of the city. The 20-ton **Pummerin bell** is a recast version of the one made from the bronze of Turkish cannons captured after the 1683 siege, but destroyed in the wartime fire of 1945. It is rung only on ceremonial occasions such as New Year's Eve.

Inside the church, in the centre aisle, is the charming carved Gothic **pulpit** of Master Anton Pilgram (1455–1515). At the head of the spiral staircase the sculptor has placed the figures of Augustine, Gregory, Jerome and Ambrose, fathers

Sculptor Master Pilgram at the foot of the organ base

of the Church – and added a sculpture of himself looking through a window under the staircase. No shrinking violet, Pilgram pops up again at the foot of the elaborate stone organ base he built in the north aisle.

Left of the high altar is the carved wooden **Wiener Neustädter Altar**. To the right is the marble **tomb** of Emperor Friedrich III (died 1493), honoured by the Viennese for having the city made a bishopric, and for inventing the *Semmel,* the little bread roll you receive with every meal.

Mass is held at 10.15am on Sunday and holidays (9.30am July and August). There are guided tours and roof walks, as well as tours of the bone-filled catacombs.

Around Stephansdom

Opposite Stephansdom looms the contrasting **Haas Haus**, a large, curved building whose windows reflect a distorted cathedral. This hinge between Graben and Stephansplatz was erected in 1990 to plans by Hans Hollein. Stephansplatz, joins Stock-im-Eisen-Platz (literally meaning 'stick set in iron'), a name which refers to a gnarled old trunk into which journeymen locksmiths arriving in medieval Vienna would drive a nail for good luck. The nails are now protected by a Perspex shield.

If you're looking for a place to relax after visiting the cathedral, walk along Rotenturmstrasse to one of the outdoor cafés on **Lugeck**, a pleasant little square where burglars used to be hanged some 300 years ago. From there, wander over to the Fleischmarkt, where, at number 11, you'll find the oldest tavern in Vienna, the **Griechenbeisl** (1490), once frequented by the likes of Mozart, Beethoven, Schubert and Strauss *(see below)*.

Around the corner on Grashofgasse, cross the courtyard of the 17th-century **Heiligenkreuzerhof** abbey to the **Basiliskenhaus** (Schönlaterngasse 7), steeped in medieval superstition. Here a basilisk – half rooster, half lizard – was said to have breathed its poisonous fumes into the drinking water, until one day a baker's apprentice held up a mirror to the monster and scared it to death.

It is a stone's throw over to the **Alte Universität** (Old University, 1365), where young Franz Schubert lived as a member of the Vienna Boys' Choir. The Alte Universität was closed down after student demonstrations in 1848 against

---

Griechenbeisl Tavern

The Griechenbeisl tavern (Fleishmarkt 11) was first recorded in 1447, but who knows how long it existed before that? Its many small vaulted rooms have been a public house ever since. First frequented by Levantine and Greek merchants (hence the name), who inhabited Fleishmarkt, it was subsequently visited by Mozart, Beethoven, Schubert, Strauss, Grillparzer and Mark Twain, among other musicians and writers. Grillparzer and Johann Strauss autographed the ceiling and Twain scribbled his short story, *The Million Dollar Bank-Note*, in the *'beisl*. It is said that in the mid-17th century, Liebe Augustin (Augustin Mitte; *O, du lieber Augustin, alles ist hin…*) played and sang here. It was customary for drinkers who consumed more than two glasses to keep a tally with matchsticks; some imbibers accumulated appreciable piles of timber.

Not content with one type of goulash, no less than 15 varieties – including tripe and chocolate – are served at GulaschMuseum (Schulerstraße 20; open daily 10am–midnight).

the autocratic regime of Metternich. The authorities moved the hotheads out of the Innere Stadt to academies in the outer districts until a new university was opened in 1884, safely on the outer edge of the Ring.

On Bäckerstrasse, the Baroque house of the old Schmauswaberl restaurant (No.16) served students cheap meals with leftovers from the Hofburg kitchens. The French lady of letters Madame de Staël lived at the Palais Seilern, and across the street (at No. 7) is a beautiful ivy-covered arcaded Renaissance courtyard.

Cut across the busy Wollzeile to Domgasse 5, where, from 1784 to 1787 Wolfgang Amadeus Mozart lived in the **Figarohaus**. In this house, now a museum (open Tues–Sun 9am–6pm; admission fee; U-Bahn 1, 3: Stephansplatz), Mozart wrote 11 piano concertos, one horn concerto, two quintets, four quartets, three trios, three piano sonatas, two violin sonatas and the opera *The Marriage of Figaro*. It is a thrill for music lovers to stand in the very room where Mozart received a respectful visit from Joseph Haydn and where the young Ludwig van Beethoven applied for music lessons. These were the great days. Four years later, around the corner in musty Rauhensteingasse, Mozart struggled to finish *The Magic Flute* and a Requiem before his time ran out. He died a pauper, his coffin assigned to an anonymous grave.

Cheer up with a stroll through the **Fähnrichshof** at the corner of Blutgasse and Singerstrasse. This charming complex of artists' studios, galleries, boutiques, apartments and gardens is a triumph of urban renovation from the total ruin left by World War II bombs. The nearby **Franziskanerplatz** presents a fine baroque ensemble – 18th-century fountain with a statue of Moses by Johann Martin Fischer, elegant Franziskanerkirche and the Kleines Café tastefully remodelled by Hermann Czech.

Kärntnerstrasse to Albertinaplatz

Kärntnerstrasse was once the city's main north–south thoroughfare, continuing on through Carinthia (Kärnten) to Trieste on the Adriatic. It has always been the central artery of Viennese social life, perhaps because it joins the sacred and the cultural heart of Vienna – the Stephansdom at one end and the Staatsoper (Opera House) at the other.

The street, which has been transformed into a traffic-free pedestrian zone, contains many of Vienna's smartest shops. Most are modern, but the Lobmeyr shop (No. 26) dates back to 1823 and now houses a **glassware museum**. The open-air cafés are an innovation in a town not hitherto noted for its street life. The Gothic **Malteserkirche** (No. 37) was founded by the crusading Knights Hospitallers.

Shopfront on Kärntnerstrasse

Just off Kärntnerstrasse, on Neuer Markt, is the **Kapuzinerkirche** (church of the Capuchin Friars). Beneath it is the 17th-century imperial burial vault, the **Kaisergruft** (open daily 9.30am–4pm; admission fee), also known as the Kapuzinergruft. Among

Sarcophagi of Franz Joseph and Sissi in the Kaisergruft

the tombs and sarcophagi of some 140 Habsburgs, note the double casket of Maria Theresa and her husband, François de Lorraine. The most recent burial was in 1989, of Zita, wife of the last emperor, Karl I (who abdicated in 1918 and is buried in Madeira). Franz Joseph and Empress Elisabeth (Sissi) are still much loved, their coffins festooned with flowers.

On Philharmonikerstrasse is the **Hotel Sacher**. If only its neoclassical walls could talk, what tales this opulent building would tell. Anna Sacher, who presided over its early days and was given to smoking large cigars, was a renowned hostess, anticipating her guests' every need. She attracted courtiers, aristocrats, diplomats and the rich, embroidering their signatures on a tablecloth. The hotel was the setting for meetings where the future of Europe was decided. And there's that chocolate cake, the *Sachertorte*, created in the 19th century for Metternich when he wanted something new and impressive for an important occasion. It went down well then, and continues to do so today.

At the intersection of Kärntnerstrasse and the Ringstrasse stands the **Staatsoper** (National Opera House). The original opera house, inaugurated in 1869, was greeted with such criticism that one of the architects, Edward van der Nüll, was driven to suicide. It was almost completely destroyed in the 1945 bombardments. The new house captures the original's neoclassical spirit.

On Albertinaplatz is the bleak **Monument Against War and Fascism** (1991) by Alfred Hrdlicka. Facing the stone gate symbolising totalitarian force is the controversial bronze sculpture of a kneeling figure, recalling the humiliation of Jews forced by the Nazi regime to scrub pavements with a toothbrush. The monument has been contested both by Jews and anti-Semites.

Albertinaplatz is also the location of the **Albertina**, the Habsburg palace that contains the **Graphische Sammlung Albertina** (Albertinaplatz 1; open daily 10am–6pm, Wed 9pm; admission fee; U-Bahn 1, 2, 4: Karlsplatz; 1, 3: Oper; tram 1, 2, J, 62, 65: Oper; <www.albertina.at>). Named after Maria Theresa's son-in-law, Duke Albert of Saxony-Teschen, and founded in 1781, this palace holds one of the world's finest collections of graphic art, with more than 60,000 original drawings and more than one million wood and copper-plate prints. The collection represents major artists from the 15th century to the present, including priceless works by Dürer, da Vinci, Michelangelo, Raphael, Titian, Rembrandt, Rubens, Van Gogh, Toulouse-Lautrec, Beardsley and Grosz.

The state rooms have recently been restored, and a new exhibition space has been built together with storage and retrieval facilities. Any of the drawings can be viewed by written request.

Monument Against War and Fascism

The oval nave of baroque Peterskirche, built in the 18th century

The Graben and the Jewish Quarter

Running northwest from Stephansplatz *(see page 25)*, the Graben, together with the adjacent Kohlmarkt and Dorotheergasse, is the centre of Vienna's most fashionable shops and coffee houses. Until the end of the Habsburgs, it was equally infamous for its Graben nymphs, as the local ladies of the night were known. The Graben and its extension, Naglergasse, mark the southern boundary of the original Roman settlement of Vindobona; the approximate square shape is completed by Rotenturmstrasse to the east, Salzgries to the north and Tiefer Graben to the west.

The Graben is now a pedestrian zone, dominated by the startling, bulbous-shaped monument to the town's deliverance from the plague in 1679. The **Pestsäule** (Plague Column) combines humility before God and gruesome fascination with the disease itself. A more joyous celebration of faith, just off the Graben, is the **Peterskirche** (St

Peter's Church), designed in 1702 by Gabriele Montani and completed by Johann Lukas von Hildebrandt. The exterior embraces the graceful oval of its nave, its rows of pews curving outwards, each decorated with three carved angels' heads. It displays the genius of Viennese Baroque for marrying the sumptuous to the intimate.

To the south of Stephansplatz, at Dorotheergasse 11, is the **Jüdisches Museum** (Jewish Museum; open Sun–Fri 10am–6pm, Thur to 8pm; admission fee; U-Bahn 1, 3: Stephansplatz; <www.jmw.at>). This comparatively recent (1993) addition to the Vienna museum scene is housed in the 18th-century Palais Eskeles, formerly the property of a prominent Jewish financier. With modern audio-visual techniques, it traces the history of the city's Jewish community from the Middle Ages, through the years of its illustrious contributions to Viennese culture, to its extermination by German and Austrian Nazis in World War II. Temporary exhibitions are also staged here, usually devoted to prominent artists, writers and other historical figures of Viennese life. Despite the community's tragic end, the museum's atmosphere is positive, reinforced by a cheerful café and bookshop on the ground floor.

The old **Jewish quarter**, still in large part a garment district, lies north of Stephansplatz and the Graben. Its medieval centre was **Judenplatz** (Jews' Square) until the progrom of 1421 *(see page 14)*, when the synagogue was dismantled and its stones carted off to build an extension to the Alte Universität. The remains of the synagogue have been excavated and now form part of the elaborate new **Judenplatz Museum Wien**, which was unveiled in 2000 and functions as an annexe to the Jüdisches Museum on Dorotheergasse *(see above)*. It also incorporates Rachel Whiteread's **Memorial to the Victims of the Holocaust** on the square. The memorial, which commemorates more than 65,000 Austrian Jews who were killed by the Nazis between 1938 and 1945, is designed so as to resemble a library turned inside out, so shelves of closed books face inwards. Around the base of the monument are the names of the camps to which Austria's Jewish population was deported.

The one **synagogue** out of the city's 24 that survived the Nazis' 1938 *Kristallnacht* pogrom is at Seitenstettengasse 4, next to a kosher restaurant (guided tours Mon–Thur 11am and 3pm; a combined ticket for the museums allows you to view the synagogue free). With its Jewish community centre, it stands behind an apartment block beside the unusual **Kornhäuselturm** (1827), studio and home of architect Josef

Ruprechtskirche, built in 1161

Kornhäusel. Inside is a drawbridge he pulled up whenever he wanted to shut himself off from his quarrelsome wife.

Around the corner is the city's oldest church, the ivy-covered Romanesque **Ruprechtskirche** (1161), which is dedicated to Rupert, patron saint of salt – a valuable commodity in earlier times. From here, cut back through Judengasse to the **Hoher Markt**. This was once the forum of Roman Vindobona, and a little museum (at No. 2) shows remains of two Roman houses laid bare by a 1945 bombardment. At the eastern end of the square is a gem of high Viennese kitsch, the **Ankeruhr**, an animated clock built in 1911 by a local insurance company. Charlemagne, Prince Eugene, Maria Theresa, Joseph Haydn and others perform their act at midday.

At the western end of Hoher Markt, turn right into Marc Aurel-Strasse, named after the Roman emperor who died in AD180. On the left, Salvatorgasse leads behind the **Altes Rathaus** (Old Town Hall) and past the superb porch of the **Salvatorkapelle**, a happy marriage of Italian Renaissance and Austrian late-Gothic sculpture. Beyond it is the slender 14th-century Gothic church of **Maria am Gestade** ('Mary on the Banks'), originally overlooking the Danube. Notice its delicate tower, the canopied porch, and remains of Gothic stained glass in the choir.

The art nouveau Ankeruhr

Platz am Hof

Walk back across the Judenplatz to the spacious **Platz am Hof**, the largest square in the old part of the city. The Babenberg dukes, predecessors of the Habsburgs, built their fortress (on the site of No. 7) in about 1150. It was both a military stronghold and a palace for festivities such as the rollicking state reception in 1165 for German emperor Friedrich Barbarossa. The **Mariensäule** (Virgin's Column) was erected in 1667 to celebrate victory over Sweden's armies in the Thirty Years' War. It was on a lamppost in the middle of this square that the revolutionaries of 1848 hanged war minister Theodor Latour. At the **Am Hof** church, a baroque reworking of a late-Gothic structure, the end of the Holy Roman Empire, said by some to be neither holy nor Roman nor an empire, was proclaimed with fanfare in 1806.

Around Herrengasse

In Bognergasse, notice the pretty *Jugendstil* façade of the **Engel-Apotheke** (1907) before returning to medieval Vienna through narrow, cobbled Naglergasse. This leads to the **Freyung** triangle, flanked by the Palais Harrach dating from 1690 (where Joseph Haydn's mother was once the family cook; now a venue for temporary exhibitions mounted by the Kunsthistorische Museum) and the **Schottenkirche** (Church of the Scots), founded by Scottish and Irish Benedictine monks in the 12th century.

To the north of the Freyung, just before the Ringstrasse, Schottengasse leads to the Mölker Bastei and the **Pasqualati-**

Platz am Hof, fronted by the elegant baroque façade of Am Hof church

haus (open Tues–Sun 9am–12.15pm and 1–4.30pm; admission fee; U-Bahn 2, 4, tram 1, 2: Schottentor). Beethoven lived in this house on several occasions between 1803 and 1815 at the invitation of his friend and patron, Baron Johann Baptist of Pasqualati. Here he composed parts of *Fidelio* and his fourth to seventh symphonies, as well as his *Piano Concerto in G-major* (Opus 58). Today it is one three Beethoven residences in Vienna open to the public as museums *(see also page 71)*.

> At Freyung 8, the Kunstforum der Bank Austria (open daily 10am–7pm, Fri 10am–9pm; admission fee; <www.kunstforum-wien.at>) mounts first-class exhibitions of contemporary art and sculpture, and paintings from the 19th and 20th centuries.

South of the Freyung is Herrengasse, the Innere Stadt's main eastbound traffic artery, lined with imposing baroque and neo-baroque palaces. Now government offices or embassies, these buildings belonged to Vienna's great Austrian, Hungarian, Italian and Czech families – Kinsky, Modena, Wilczek, Pallavicini and Batthyaninow.

Here, too, is the 18th-century **Palais Ferstel**, incorporating an elegant shopping arcade, Freyung Passage, and the restored **Café Central**, Vienna's leading coffee house before World War I *(see page 95)*. Upstairs, a restaurant occupies the gilded premises of the old stock exchange.

Herrengasse leads to Michaelerplatz and the Hofburg *(see page 40)*. Once the imperial parish church, **Michaelerkirche** is a hybrid mixture of Romanesque, Gothic and baroque. At No. 5 is the architecturally revolutionary **Looshaus**, now a bank. Built by Adolf Loos, its starkly functional use of fine materials shocked many in 1910. Emperor Franz Joseph so hated its 'outrageously naked' façade that he stopped using the Hofburg's Michaelertor exit.

The Vienna Boys' Choir in the Schweizerhof

THE HOFBURG

Defeat in war took away the Habsburgs, but not the palaces. They remain to warm the cockles of Vienna's imperial heart. Most imposing is the **Hofburg** (Michaelerplatz 1; open Wed–Mon 10am–4pm; admission fee; U-Bahn 2: Babenbergerstrasse or Herrengasse; tram 1, 2, D, J: Burgring), home of Austria's rulers since the 13th century. It covers the southwest corner of the Innere Stadt.

The vast palace went through five major stages of construction over six centuries, and at the end there was still a large unfinished section. Today, the palace's museums exhibit most of the vast personal fortune of the Habsburgs.

Imperial Apartments

To sense the human scale of the Habsburgs' gigantic enterprise, start by taking the 45-minute guided tour of the **Kaiserappartements** (Imperial Apartments). Coming from the Michaelerplatz, the entrance is to the left of the Hofburg rotunda. You will see splendid Gobelins tapestries; a smoking room for the emperor's fellow officers; enormous rococo stoves needed to heat the place; a crystal chandelier weighing half a tonne; Franz Joseph's austere bedroom with iron military camp-bed; and rooms used by his wife, Elisabeth (Sissi), including her newly restored drawing room and bedroom, and the gymnasium she used for daily exercise, complete with wall bars and climbing ropes.

The first six rooms, the so-called Stephansappartement, are devoted to the **Sissi Museum**, which examines the life of the empress from her carefree childhood in Bavaria to her cruel murder at the hands of an anarchist in Geneva. Particular emphasis is placed on the private life of Elisabeth, including her exercise regimes and obsession with beauty.

The Life and Death of an Empress

Elisabeth, affectionately known as Sissi, was a Bavarian Princess and a legend in both her own lifetime and more than a century after her death. She married Emperor Franz Joseph 1 in 1854 when she was just 16. She was never at home with the oppressive formality of court life; despite this, her presence made the court the most glittering in Europe. She was noted for her stringent exercise and beauty regime. Hair care took hours, and Elisabeth's hairdresser was a confidante who sometimes took her mistress's place during boring functions where the empress would not be closely scrutinised.

As she grew older, Sissi was able to lead her own life, travelling extensively. She loved the imperial train. In 1898, at the age of 60, she was fatally stabbed by an Italian anarchist in Geneva. In Austria and Hungary she is still a figure of enchantment. A Winterhalter portrait of Sissi with stars in her hair, old romantic films and, most recently, a musical about her life have, perhaps, kept memories green.

Imperial Silver Collection

To the right of the Hofburg rotunda coming from the Michaelerplatz is the **Hofsilber und Tafelkammer** (Court Imperial Silver and Tableware Collection). On display here are the priceless Chinese, Japanese, French Sèvres and German Meissen services amassed by the Habsburgs over six centuries of weddings and birthdays. Highlights are a 140-piece service in vermeil and a neo-Renaissance centrepiece given to Emperor Franz Joseph by Queen Victoria in 1851.

The Stallburg

In 1533, four years after the Turks were repulsed, Ferdinand I felt safe enough to settle in the Hofburg, bringing his barons and bureaucrats to make their homes in nearby Herrengasse and Wallnerstrasse. He built the **Stallburg** in 1565 (outside the main Hofburg complex on Reitschulgasse) as a home for his son Archduke Maximilian. It was subsequently turned into stables for the horses of the Spanish Riding School. With its fine three-storey arcaded courtyard, the Stallburg is the most important Renaissance building in Vienna. The stables are no longer open to the public, but visitors can see into six of the 68 stalls from behind a glass screen in the **Lipizzaner Museum** next door (open daily 9am–6pm).

In the first half of the 18th-century, Imperial Vienna was transformed into a city of the baroque. This was largely the work of three Austrian architects: Johann Bernhard Fischer von Erlach, his son Josef Emanuel, and Johann Lukas von Hildebrandt.

Spanish Riding School

Part of the massive expansion of the Hofburg that took place in the 17th and 18th centuries is the magnificent parade hall of the **Wintereitschule**, home of the **Spanische Reitschule** (Spanish Riding School), right opposite the Stallburg. It is worth visiting on architectural grounds alone: constructed between 1729 and 1735, it is the work of Josef Emanuel Fischer von Erlach and is considered a masterpiece of the baroque.

The Lipizzaner horses perform in its elegant arena throughout the year, except in July and August. Tickets must be booked well in advance (write to Spanische Reitschule, Michaelerplatz 1, A–1010 Vienna, tel 431 533 90 31). A cheaper option is to watch the horses

A Lipizzaner performing at the Spanish Riding School

train. Morning exercises are held between 10am and noon Tuesday to Saturday (except in July and August). Tickets are sold from 9am at the Visitor Centre, Michaelerplatz 1 (reservations cannot be made). The Lipizzaners, originally a Spanish breed, were raised at Lipica in Slovenia, not far from Trieste; since 1920 the tradition has been carried on in the Styrian town of Piber. By methods that have not changed since the 17th century, the horses are trained to walk and dance with a delicacy that many ballet dancers would envy. They perform classical figures to the music of the polka, gavotte, quadrille – and the Viennese waltz. Another world in another age is recalled as these shining white horses with gold ribbons tied into their plaited manes and tails are led in by equerries wearing cocked hats, brown tailcoats edged with black silk, white buckskin breeches, sabres and riding boots. Custom demands that gentlemen take their hats off when the equerries enter. The spectacle more than merits the gesture.

National Library

Beside the Spanish Riding School complex is **Josefsplatz**, a marvellously harmonious Baroque square, in the middle of which stands Franz Anton Zauner's equestrian statue (1795–1807) of Emperor Joseph II.

The Great Hall of the National Library

Behind is the main building of the **Österreichische Nationalbibliothek** (Austrian National Library), which contains more than 2 million manuscripts and printed books, maps, portraits, musical scores, papyrus documents and a globe museum. The building – the former Imperial Library – is one of the most important works of the court architect Johann Bernhard Fischer von Erlach; it was constructed between 1723 and 1735 under the supervision of his son, Josef Emanuel. The highlight is the **Prunksaal** (Great Hall; open May–Oct daily 10am–4pm, Thur 7pm; Nov–Apr daily 10am–2pm, Thur 7pm; admission fee), one of the world's greatest secular baroque interiors. The ceiling frescoes (1730) by Daniel Gran depict the apotheosis of the library's founder, Emperor Charles VI.

The baroque **Augustinerkirche** was the Habsburgs' wedding church. It was here that Maria Theresa married François of Lorraine in 1736, Marie-Louise married Napoleon *(in absentia)* in 1810, and Franz Joseph married Elisabeth in 1854. Although the Habsburgs' burial church is the Kapuzinerkirche over on Neuer Markt *(see page 31)*, the heart of the deceased was buried deep in the Augustiner crypt.

Schweizerhof

The **Schweizerhof** (The Swiss Court), the oldest part of the Hofburg, is named after the Swiss Guard once housed there. Here King Ottokar of Bohemia built a fortress in 1275 to resist Rudolf von Habsburg. Victorious Rudolf moved in and strengthened the fortifications to keep out the unruly Viennese. By the archway are the pulleys for the chains of the drawbridge. But Rudolf's son, Albrecht I, preferred the safety of Leopoldsberg in the Vienna Woods. For 250 years, the fortress was used only for ceremonial occasions. The **Burgkapelle** (Castle Chapel) was built in 1449. Originally Gothic, it was redone in baroque style and then partially restored to its original form in 1802. It's here that the famous Wiener Sängerknaben (Vienna Boys' Choir) sings Mass.

In the Schweizerhof, the **Schatzkammer** (treasury) contains a dazzling display of the insignia of the old Holy Roman

Vienna Boys' Choir

The Wiener Sängerknaben (Vienna Boys' Choir) was founded in 1498 as part of the Imperial Chapel choir with 16 to 20 choirboys. It increased steadily in size over the years, and in the 18th and 19th centuries included Josef Haydn and Franz Schubert among its members. Re-established in 1924, it today consists of four individual choirs, each having 24 members.

The choir sings Mass on Sunday and church festivals in the Burgkapelle (tickets must be booked in advance). It also performs occasional mixed programmes of motets, madrigals, waltz music and folk songs in the Musikverein *(see page 83)*. For further information, see <www.wsk.at> or tel: 431 216 39 42.

The crown, orb and sceptre of the Holy Roman Empire

Empire. Highlights are the Imperial Crown of pure unalloyed gold set with pearls and unpolished emeralds, sapphires and rubies. First used in AD962 for the coronation of Otto the Great in Rome, it moved on to Aachen and Frankfurt for crowning successors. Also on display are the sword of Charlemagne and the Holy Lance, which is said to have pierced the body of Christ on the Cross and which has been claimed by some, including Hitler, to have mystical powers. Other intriguing artefacts include a unicorn's horn; a 'viper tongue credenza' used to render poisoned food edible; and an agate bowl, reputed to be the Holy Grail used by Christ at the Last Supper.

In der Burg

The Schweizertor (Swiss Gate) leads into the busy square known as **In der Burg**, which is surrounded by buildings from various eras. Leopold I launched the city's baroque era with his **Leopoldinischer Trakt** (Leopoldine Wing) – a residence in keeping with the Habsburgs' role as a world power. Constructed in 1660–66 by Domenico and Martin Carlone, in accordance with a design by Philiberto Luchesi, it serves today as the official residence of the president of Austria.

The **Amalienburg**, which was started under Emperor Maximilian II in the early-baroque style, was finished in 1611 during the reign of Emperor Rudolf II by Pietro Ferrabosco and Antonio de Moys. It was named after Amalia of Brunswick, the consort of Emperor Joseph I.

The **Reichskanzleitrakt** housed the imperial administration until 1806. It was designed by Johann Lukas von Hildebrandt and Josef Emanuel Fischer von Erlach between 1723 and 1730; the four sculptures (*The Labours of Hercules*) are the work of Lorenzo Mattielli who was active at the same time.

Neue Burg

A passage leads from In der Burg to spacious **Heldenplatz** (Heroes Square). At the end of the 19th century, Franz Joseph embarked on building a gigantic Kaiser Forum. This was to have embraced the vast Heldenplatz (Heroes' Square) with two crescent-shaped arms, the whole extending through triumphal arches to the Naturhistorisches and Kunsthistorisches museums. Only the first of the two crescents, the **Neue Burg** was built before the empire collapsed. Today, it houses a congress centre, several museums, and reading rooms for the National Library.

It contains perhaps the most Viennese of all collections in the Hofburg, the exquisite **Sammlung alter Musikinstrumente** (Musical Instruments Collection; open Mon, Wed–Sun 10am–6pm; admission fee), comprising 360 pieces including Renaissance instruments representing practically everything played up to the 17th century. Also on view are Haydn's harpsichord, Beethoven's piano of 1803 and an 1839 piano used by Schumann and Brahms.

The Burggarten and its Jugendstil Palmenhaus

The Burggarten

The **Burggarten**, the Hofburg's park, was laid out for the imperial family in the early 19th century. It has monuments to Franz Joseph I (1908, by Klimbusch) and Mozart (1896, by Viktor Tilgner). There is also the early 20th-century *Jugendstil* Palmenhaus (glass house) by Friedrich Ohmann. This contains a lovely café, and the Schmetterlinghaus, a butterfly garden (open Mon–Fri 10am–5pm, Sat–Sun 10am–6.30pm).

RINGSTRASSE AND ITS MUSEUMS

After the Hofburg, take a walk (or tram ride) around the Ringstrasse, the single urban achievement of Franz Joseph. This boulevard encircling the Innere Stadt was created in the 1860s along the route of the old city walls. Inspired by what the emperor had seen on a visit to Paris, the project captured the energetic spirit of the times. The neoclassical buildings bring together all the great architectural styles of Europe's past.

Start west of the Schottenring, at the **Votivkirche**, a neo-Gothic church built after Franz Joseph survived an assassination attempt in 1853. Next to it are the university and **Rathaus** (Town Hall). Proceed along Dr-Karl-Lueger-Ring, and on the Innere Stadt side is the imposing **Burgtheater** *(see page 84)*, a high temple of German theatre. Beyond is the lovely **Volksgarten**, with its small buildings and scaled-down copy of the Athenian Temple of Theseus. Its cafés and concerts carry on a tradition that began with the café music of the Strauss family.

Opposite is the temple-like **Parlament**, built by Theophil Hansen after a long stay in Athens. The ring bends to become the Burg Ring, flanked on the Innere Stadt side by the Hofburg and on the other side by **Maria-Theresien-Platz**, which lies betewen the Kunsistorisches Museum and Naturhistorisches Museum

Kunsthistorisches Museum

If the **Kunsthistorisches Museum** (Museum of Fine Arts; open Tues-Sun 10am–6pm, Thur until 9pm; admission fee; U-Bahn 2: Babenberger-strasse; tram D, J, 1, 2: Bur-gring; wheelchair access Burgring 5; <www.khm.at>) is less well-known than the Louvre or the Prado, it may just be that the name is something of a mouthful. The collection is, quite simply, magnificent. Bene-fiting from the cultural diversity of the Habsburg Empire, it in fact encom-passes a much broader spec-

Kunsthistorisches Museum – the main staircase

Madonna of the Meadows,
by Raphael

trum of Western European art than many of its better-known counterparts. The **Gemäldegalerie** (Gallery of Paintings) on the first floor displays a dazzling array of European art from the 16th to 18th centuries. Dutch, Flemish, German and English works are in the east wing, left of the main entrance, and Italian, Spanish and French works in the west wing, to the right. Whatever your taste, you can't fail to be awestruck: there are masterpieces by Caravaggio, Dürer, Raphael, Rembrandt, Rubens, Titian, Velasquez, Vermeer, and an entire room devoted to Breughel.

The lower floor contains an impressive collection of ancient Egyptian, Greek and Roman art, as well as the **Sculpture and Applied Arts Collection**, whose prized possession is Benvenuto Cellini's famous gold-enamelled **salt cellar** made for King François I of France. The highlight of the **Classical Antiquities Collection** is the exquisite **Gemma Augustea**, a 1st-century onyx cameo. The **Egyptian/Oriental Collection** contains, among other treasures, the burial chamber of Prince Kaninisut. The top floor of the museum holds the **Secondary Gallery** of paintings and the **Numismatic Collection**.

Also part of the Kunsthistorisches Museum is the **Ephesus Museum** (open Mon, Wed–Sun 10am–6pm; admission fee), housed in the Neue Burg *(see page 47)* and displaying items from a long interest in that city; Austrian archaeologists have been working there since 1866.

Naturhistorisches Museum

The architectural twin to the Kunsthistorisches Museum stands opposite: the **Naturhistorisches Museum** (Natural History Museum; open Wed–Mon, 9am–6.30pm, Wed till 9pm; admission fee; U-Bahn 2, 3: Volkstheater; tram D, J, 1, 2: Dr Karl-Renner-Ring; <www.nhm-wien.at>) The museum contains exhibits ranging from insects to dinosaurs, and an impressive collection of meteorites. The vast reserves derive in part from the private collections of François de Lorraine (1708–65), husband of Maria Theresa. Highlights include the 25,000-year-old figurine, *Venus of Willendorf*, a 117-kg (260-lb) giant topaz, and Maria Theresa's exquisite jewel bouquet made of precious stones. The Kindersaal (Children's Room) is a great family attraction.

MuseumsQuartier

At the other side of Museumstrasse is the modern museum complex, the **Museums-Quartier** (Visitor and Ticket Centre, Museumsplatz, open daily 10am–7pm; U-Bahn 2, 3: Volkstheater; <www.mqw. at>). Comprising Fischer von Erlach's 18th-century former Hofstallungen (imperial stables) alongside stunning new buildings, it is home to **MUMOK** (the Museum of Modern Art) with its impressive collection of 20th-century work by artists such as

The Leopold Museum in the MuseumsQuartier

The Secessionsgebäude

Kandinsky, Ernst, Magritte and Warhol; the **Leopold Museum** (closed Tues) featuring Austrian art from the 19th and 20th centuries; **Architekturzentrum Wien** (Vienna Architecture Centre); and the **Tabak Museum** (Tobacco Museum; closed Mon). Contemporary art exhibitions are on show in **Kunsthalle Wien** (closed Tues). The **Zoom Kindermuseum** is devoted to interactive education.

Fine Arts Academy

The Ringstrasse bends round to become the Opern Ring. On the right is Schillerplatz, home to the **Akademie der Bildenden Künste** (Academy of Fine Arts; open Tues–Sun 10am–6pm; admission fee; U-Bahn 1, 2, 4: Karlsplatz/Oper; tram 1, 2, D, J; <www. akbild.ac.at>). Few art academies can rival its outstanding collection of European paintings – particularly Dutch and Flemish masters – from the 14th century to the present day. Highlights include *The Last Judgment* by Hieronymus Bosch and works by Rubens, Rembrandt, Van Dyck, Pieter de Hooch and Tiepolo. The building itself was constructed in the 1870s to an Italian Renaissance design by Theophil Hansen.

Secessionsgebäude

Standing defiantly opposite, on the corner of Friedrichstrasse, is the distinctive **Secessionsgebäude** (Secession Building; open Tues–Sat 10am–6pm, Sun 10am–4pm;

admission fee; U-Bahn 1, 2, 4: Karlsplatz; tram 1, 2, D, J; <www. secession.at>). This is the gallery of the Secession Movement, which was formed when 19 artists (the most celebrated being Gustav Klimt) broke from what they saw as the reactionary Viennese art establishment in 1897. It was built by Josef Maria Olbrich, a student of Otto Wagner. An inscription above the door proclaims: *'Der Zeit ihre Kunst, der Kunst ihre Freiheit'* ('To the Age, its own Art; to Art, its own Freedom'). The building is topped with a golden dome of laurel leaves, aptly known as the golden cabbage and said to symbolise the interdependence of art and nature. Contemporary work is also on show. In the basement is Klimt's magnificent *Beethoven Frieze,* created for a Secession exhibition in 1902. The largest collection of Klimt's paintings is in the Austrian Gallery in the Upper Belvedere *(see page 60)*.

Jugendstil

In Austria, *Jugendstil* (art nouveau) caught the imagination of the art world, and the result was the foundation of the Secession Movement by a group of renegade artists from the Academy in 1897. The central figure of the Secession was Gustav Klimt (1862–1918), whose erotic, fairytale-like painting and themes came to embody *Jugendstil.* One of the key tenets for artists such as Klimt and Koloman Moser, and the leading *Jugendstil* architects Otto Wagner and Josef Hoffmann, was the linking of function and aesthetic.

Klimt's decorative elegance was a particular source of inspiration for Egon Schiele (1890–1918), whose linearity and subtlety reveals the strong influence of the *Jugendstil.* Schiele, however, emphasised expression over decoration, concentrating on the human figure with an acute eroticism that was less decorative than Klimt's. Evocation of intense feeling through colours and lines was of equal importance to Oskar Kokoschka (1886–1980), a leading exponent of Expressionism.

Contrasting styles, Karlsplatz

Karlsplatz

There are a number of attractions on and around nearby **Karlsplatz**. The elegant glass cube on Treitlstrasse is called **Project Space** (open daily 1–7pm; admission fee; U-Bahn 1, 2, 4), a branch of the Kunsthalle Wien (in the MuseumsQuartier), which stages exhibitions featuring topical themes and current trends in contemporary art. The café, with its giant terrace, is a great meeting place for young people (and those young at heart).

The square is dominated by the huge **Karlskirche**, the most important of the city's baroque churches. It was built by Fischer von Erlach for Karl VI, fulfilling an oath made by the emperor during the plague of 1713. Sunset offers a spectacular view of the big dome across the Karlsplatz. The cool, sober interior has a subdued marble decor and spacious oval ground plan similar to that of the Peterskirche *(see page 34)*. The oval dome's ceiling **frescoes** are by Johann Michael Rottmayr, the *trompe-l'oeil* by Gaetano Fanti. Notice, too, Naiel Gran's lovely painting of **St Elisabeth** in the main chapel on the right. In front of the church, Henry Moore's sculpture *Hill Arches* provides a striking contrast.

At the eastern end of Karlsplatz is **Historisches Museum der Stadt Wien** (Vienna City History Museum; open Tues–Sun 9am–6pm; admission fee; U-Bahn 1, 2, 4: Karlsplatz; <www.museum-vienna.at>). Displays cover the major historical events in the city, from the siege in 1529 to the modern artistic movements. Opposite is the magnificent neoclassical building of the **Musikverein** (Society of the

Friends of Music, *see page 83*). Constructed in 1867 to a design by Theophil Hansen, it is home to the Vienna Philharmonic Orchestra. The ceiling paintings, *Apollo and the Nine
Muses* (1911), are by August Eisenmenger.

Beside the Academy of Music lies the **Künstlerhaus**
(1868), which houses art exhibitions (open Fri–Wed
10am–6pm, Thur 10am–9pm; <www.k-haus.at>). In front is
Otto Wagner's **Stadtbahn Pavilion** (Municipal Railway
Pavilion), with its graceful green, gold and white motif of
sunflowers and tulips.

Across the Kärntner Ring, the road becomes the Schubert
and then the Park Ring as it passes **Stadtpark**. The park is
home to the famous glittering bronze and marble monument
to Strauss the Younger, and also monuments to other Austrians of note, including Schubert and Brückner. The Café
Hubner is set among the trees.

Stadtbahn Pavilion by Secession architect Otto Wagner

Applied Art Museum

On the same side of the Ring, across Weiskirchnerstrasse is the **Museum für Angewandte Kunst** (Museum for Applied Art; open Tues–Sun 10am–6pm; Tues until midnight; admission fee, Sat free; U-Bahn 3, tram 1, 2: Stubentor; U-Bahn 4: Landstrasse; <www.mak.at>). Known simply as MAK, this is one of the city's most exciting and thought-provoking museums, The exhibition rooms are designed by contemporary artists who often reveal unexpected other sides to quite mundane objects, such as Michael Thonet's shadow play on bentwood chairs; you'll never view dining chairs in quite the same way again. There's a chance to see some particularly Viennese Biedermeier furnishings, as well as a collection of East Asian and Islamic art. The museum shop has a selection of items – design conscious, arty and some downright humorous. Opposite the museum is De Karl Lueger-Platz.

Biedermeier

The architecture, furniture and interior decoration known as 'Biedermeier' was produced in the period following Napoleon's defeat, between the Congress of Vienna in 1815 and the revolution in 1848. It was a time of political suppression in which the middle classes turned their attention to the arts. Biedermeier began as a satire, poking fun at the plodding German middle class. Two authors, Ludwig Eichrodt and Adolf Kussmaul, wrote poems in a journal called *Fliegende Blatter*, purporting to be the works of the unsophisticated 'Biedermeier', who, with his chum 'Bummelmeier', were boringly conventional. The name became synonymous with the age, but the work produced was far from dull. The Villa Wertheimstein *(see page 71)* and Dreimäderlhaus (Schreyvogelgasse 10) are fine examples of Biedermeier architecture; furniture is on display in the Museum of Applied Art *(see above)*; and pieces can still be found in antiques shops.

Dominating the centre is the memorial to Dr Karl Lueger, the popular mayor of Vienna (1897–1910) who is remembered for impoving the lot of the working class and developing Vienna as a modern city. The neighbouring **Café Pruckl** is a welcome sight if you need a break. The Stubenring passes near the **Postsparkassenamt** (Savings Bank), another masterpiece of the Secession by Otto Wagner.

OUTSIDE THE RING

The Innere Stadt and the Ringstrasse by no means have a monopoly on sights. There's plenty more to be seen outside the Ring, from royal palaces to an Undertaker's Museum.

Hundertwasser Haus

Dismissed by architectural purists as a bit of a joke, the whimsical **Hundertwasser Haus** is a hugely popular tourist attraction This public housing complex in Kegelgasse was designed by Austria's best-known artist of recent tmes, Friedensreich Hundertwasser (1928–2000). The undulating façades of 52 apartments are decorated with bright paintwork, tiles, ceramics and onion domes. Hundertwasser was a master of whimsy, and had an individual philosophy. He was opposed to the

Friedensreich Hundertwasser's Kunsthaus Wien

An idea of the depth of Hundertwasser's concern for the environment can be gained from a visit to the Fernwärmewerk at Spittelau (U-Bahn: Spittelau; free guided tours), a rubbish-incinerator whose entire emissions output is used to heat 60,000 homes. It is crowned by a vast image of the artist's cap. The mayor and citizens of Osaka, Japan, liked it so much, they installed their own Hundert-wasser-style incinerator on a specially created island in their city.

tyranny of straight lines and was the antithesis of the brutal, rigid, concrete school: Hundertwasser buildings look as if they just grew organically, and the tenants include trees.

In the nearby Untere Weissgerberstrasse is Hundertwasser's own museum, the eccentric **Kunsthaus Wien** (open daily 10am–7pm; tram N, 0: Radetzky-platz; wheelchair access; <www.kunsthauswien.com>), which is devoted to the 20th-century artist's own colourful works and changing exhibitions of work by his contemporaries.

Belvedere

The summer palace of Prince Eugene of Savoy is regarded as the finest flower of Vienna's baroque residential architecture. Though close to the Innere Stadt, in the Third District, the **Belvedere** (museums open Tues–Sun 10am–6pm, winter till 5pm; admission fee; Oberes Belvedere, Prinz-Eugene-Strasse 27, tram D; Unteres Belvedere, Renweg 6a, tram 71; <www.belvedere.at>) is an enchanted world apart with its allegorical sculptures, fountains, waterfalls and gardens.

The **Unteres** (Lower) **Belvedere** was built by Johann Lukas von Hildebrandt in 1714–16, and served as Prince Eugene's summer residence. (His winter palace is another jewel now brightening the lives of bureaucrats in the

Finance Ministry on Himmelpfortgasse.) The palace was acquired by Maria Theresa after the prince's death, and was used by various members of the Habsburg dynasty, including Archduke Franz Ferdinand, whose assassination at Sarajevo in 1914 sparked World War I. In 1955, the four victorious powers of World War II met in the Upper Belvedere to sign the treaty for Austria's independence as a neutral country.

Today the Lower Belvedere houses the **Österreichisches Barockmuseum** (Museum of Austrian Baroque Art), which presents the epitome of 18th-century Vienna with warm portraits of Maria Theresa and her husband François de Lorraine. It includes paintings by Gran, Maulbertsch and Rottmayr, and sculpture by Donner and Permoser, most notably the latter's *Apotheosis of Prince Eugene*, which forms the centrepiece of the highly ornate rococo

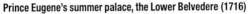

Prince Eugene's summer palace, the Lower Belvedere (1716)

gilt and mirrored Golden Cabinet. Commissioned by the prince himself, it shows Eugene as Hercules spurning Envy and trying to silence Fame's trumpet.

The palace's **Orangerie** (access through the Lower Belvedere) is home to the **Museum Mittelalterlicher Österreichischer Kunst** (Museum of Medieval Austrian Art), which includes some fine examples of 15th-century statuary and altarpieces from the Tyrol, Salzburg, Lower Austria and Styria.

Prince Eugene held banquets and other festivities in the **Oberes** (Upper) **Belvedere**, completed in 1723. Today it houses **Österreichische Galerie des 19. und 20. Jahrhunderts** (Austrian Gallery of

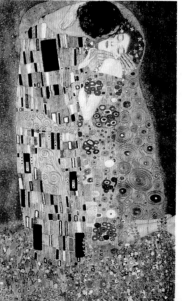

The Kiss, by Gustav Klimt

the 19th and 20th Centuries). The gallery reflects the Austro-Hungarian Empire's image as a declining world power, culminating in a final grand artistic fling around 1900. Most of the art thus produced is displayed on the first floor, and includes such masterpieces as *The Kiss* by Gustav Klimt. Egon Schiele and Oskar Kokoschka are well represented, and there is a small but stunning collection of Impressionist and post-Impressionist art, featuring works by Monet, Renoir, Cézanne, Van Gogh and Edvard Munch, and sculptures by Rodin, Degas and Renoir. The Upper Belvedere **terrace** offers a splendid panoramic view of the city skyline, remarkably little changed since Bellotto-Canaletto painted it in 1760. For your walk through the gardens, the best place to start is at the Oberes Belvedere. The sunset view is a pure delight.

Bestattungsmuseum

Across Prinz-Eugene-Strasse from the Oberes Belvedere, at Goldeggasse 19, is the typically Viennese **Bestattungs-museum** (Undertaker's Museum; open Mon–Fri noon–3pm; admission fee; tram D; <www.bestattungwien.at>). Here you can learn all there is to learn about such devices as reusable coffins (after the ceremony, the hinged flaps would open and the corpse was left behind while the coffin was taken off to be used again). The museum's ashtrays are inscribed *Rauchen sichert Arbeitsplatze* (smoking guarantees jobs). And who but the Viennese (it was recently reported) would invent a solar-powered glow-in-the dark-tombstone?

Zentralfriedhof

The Viennese, it must be said, do not consider it morbid to be interested in funerals and admire *eine schöne Leich* (a fine corpse). They enjoy a walk through the **Zentralfriedhof** (Central Cemetery, Simmeringer Hauptstrasse 234; tram 71, 72.) The recorded voice on the tram announces: 'Central Cemetery, Last stop! Everybody out!' Opened in 1874, the cemetery has 200 hectares (500 acres) of handsome or kitsch funerary monuments that pay homage to the city's great: Beethoven, Schubert, Brahms, Schönberg, and writers Arthur Schnitzel and Franz Werfel. Look for the memorial to Mozart, buried elsewhere in an unmarked pauper's grave. A detailed map of the cemetery is available at Tor (Gate) 2.

G-Town

Also situated in the south of the city are the **Simmering Gasometers** (U-Bahn 3: Gasometer; <www.g-town.at>). These four gasholders were built for the city in 1896–9. Although functional structures, they were brick-built with their own distinctive aesthetic quality. Following their decommissioning in 1986, a scheme was launched to give the gasometers a new lease of life. The results are worth seeing: now known as G-town, the complex opened in 2001. Walkways lead between the structures, which contain a shopping mall with 70 shops and 20

Gasometer interior

restaurants, cafés and bars. Attached is a colourful entertainment centre with a multi-screen cinema and a hall seating 4,200 people, and there are also offices, flats, student accommodation and the Vienna National Archives here.

Shopping and Museums

To the west of the Ringstrasse, leading out from the MuseumsQuartier *(see page 51)*, is **Mariahilferstrasse**, the city's most popular shopping street. Parallel to this is Gumpendorfer Strasse, where **Café Sperl** at No. 11 is a well-known cultural landmark. Just to the south, along the Linke Wienzeile, are the fruit, vegetable and meat stalls of the famous **Naschmarkt** (food market), which has been here since the

16th century. Originally it was beside a river, the Wienfluss. In the 19th century the river was roofed over and stalls set up on the roof – so while you are wandering, you are walking over water. There are plenty of places for lunch here. Notice the *Jugendstil* façade of **Majolikahaus** at No. 40, by Secessionist architect Otto Wagner. Nearby is the venerable **Theater an der Wien**, built in 1801 for the impressario Emanuel Schikaneder, the librettist of Mozart's *Magic Flute*.

Further west, is the **Haydn Museum** (Haydngasse 19; open Tues–Sun 9am–12.15pm, 1pm–4.30pm; admission fee; U-Bahn 3: Zieglergasse). This is where the composer lived from 1797 until his death on 31 May 1809. His two oratorios *The Creation* and *The Seasons* were conceived and written in this house.

North of the Innere Stadt, at Berggasse 19, is the **Sigmund Freud Museum** (open July–Sept 9am–6pm, Oct–June 9am–5pm; admission fee; tram D: Schlickgasse), dedicated to the father of psychoanalysis. His Vienna home is a mecca for practitioners, students and patients of psychoanalysis. Freud lived here from 1891 until the arrival of the Nazis in 1938. A photograph shows the house draped with a swastika. All has been faithfully reconstituted by his disciples, with original furniture and belongings, including his hats, walking stick and suitcases initialled S.F.

Vienna's renowned Naschmarkt

The **Schubert Museum** at Nussdorferstrasse 54 (open Tues–Sun 9am–12.15pm, 1pm–4.30pm; admission fee; tram 37, 38: Canisiusgasse) is set in the house where the composer was born in 1797.

Schloss Schönbrunn, the imperial palace of Maria Theresa

SCHÖNBRUNN

Affairs of state were not something Maria Theresa ran away from, but she did prefer to handle them in the calmer setting of **Schönbrunn** (open Nov–Mar daily 8.30am–4.30pm, Apr–June, Sept, Oct 8.30am–5pm; Aug 8.30am–6pm; admission fee; U-Bahn 4: Schönbrunn; tram 10, 58; bus 10A; <www.schoenbrunn.at>). As soon as she was settled on the throne in 1740, she moved into the palace Leopold I built as a summer residence and which her father, Karl VI, had used as a lodge for pheasant shoots.

If the Hofburg is the oversized expression of a dynasty that outgrew itself, Schönbrunn is the smiling, serene expression of the personality of one woman, imperial nonetheless. Finding Fischer von Erlach's various ideas for designing a 'super Versailles' too pompous, Maria Theresa brought in her favourite architect, Nikolaus Pacassi. He made Schönbrunn an imposing edifice, creating warm and decorative rococo interiors, which were a symbol of Maria Theresa's 'idyllic absolutism'.

The Gardens

To appreciate Schönbrunn's tendency to pleasure rather than imperial pomp, visit the **gardens** first. With the exception of the Kammergarten (Chamber Garden) and Kronprinzengarten (Crown Prince Garden) immediately left and right of the palace, the park has always been open to the public. Maria Theresa liked to have her Viennese around her. The park, laid out in classical French manner, is dominated by the **Gloriette,** a neoclassical colonnade perched on the crest of a hill. It is difficult to say which view is prettier – the graceful silhouette of the Gloriette against a sunset viewed from the palace, or a bright morning view from the Gloriette over the whole of Vienna to the north and the Wienerwald to the south.

On the way to the Gloriette you will pass the Neptune Fountain and countless other statues of ancient mythology. East of the fountain are the half-buried artificial **'Roman ruins'**, built by von Hohenberg in 1778, complete with fragmented Corinthian columns, friezes and archways. Nearby is the Schöner Brunnen, the 'beautiful spring' discovered by Emperor Matthias around 1615, from which the palace took its name and which provided the water supply.

Schönbrunn garden walkway

West of Neptune is a **zoo** (open daily Nov–Jan 9am–4.30pm, Feb 9am–5pm, Apr 9am–6pm, May–Sept 9am–

6.30pm; admission fee), established in 1752 by François de Lorraine, the consort of Maria Theresa. The pandas given to the zoo in 2003 are a popular attraction. After the zoo, you can lose yourself in the topiary **maze** and a **Tyrolean Garden** (with a café). Other attractions include the **Palmenhaus** (Palm House) and **Wüstenhaus** (Desert Experience House; both open 1 May–30 Sept 9.30am–5.30pm, Oct–Apr 9.30am –4.30pm; admission fee).

The Palace

Crossing the courtyard to the palace's front entrance, you'll see on the right the **Schlosstheater**, now the site of summer chamber opera performances. In 1908, Franz Joseph's 60th anniversary as emperor was celebrated here with a ballet that included 43 Habsburg archdukes and archduchesses, aged 3 to 18.

Schönbrunn sculpture

A conducted tour of the **palace** reveals something of the cosy ambience enjoyed by Maria Theresa and her successors: her breakfast room, decorated with the needlework of the empress and her myriad daughters; the **Spiegelsaal** (Hall of Mirrors), in which the young Mozart gave his first royal recital; the **Chinesisches Rundkabinett** (Chinese Round Room), also known as Maria Theresa's

Konspirationstafelstube ('top secret dining room'). For her secret consultations, a table rose from the floor with a completely prepared dinner so that no servants would be present during the conversation. Guests used the **billiard room** while awaiting an audience with Franz Joseph. He, too, preferred Schönbrunn to the Hofburg and kept his mistress, actress Katharina Schratt, in a villa in the neighbouring district of Hietzing. Also on view is the bedroom where he died on 30 November 1916, at the age of 86.

The most ornate room at Schönbrunn is known as the MillionsRoom, with walls panelled in costly rosewood in the rococo style. Gilt-edged cartouches set into wood contain Indian miniature paintings showing the court and private lives of the 16th- and 17th-century Moghul emperors. To make them fit, original paintings were cut up by members of the Imperial family and arranged as collages to form new pictures.

The stately and the human are poignantly juxtaposed in the opulence of the ballrooms and dining rooms and the intimacy of the living quarters. The **Napoleon Room** (originally Maria Theresa's bedroom) was used by the French emperor on his way to victory at Austerlitz and by his son, the Duke of Reichstadt, in his final sad years. It is both pathetic and awesome to sense Napoleon's presence in a room that now contains his son's death mask and stuffed pet bird. Down the corridor, the last Habsburg abdicated at the end of World War I and Kennedy and Khrushchev met for dinner at the height of the Cold War. In the adjoining **Wagenburg Museum** (open Apr–Oct daily 9am–6pm, Nov–Mar Tues–Sun 10am–4pm; admission fee) you can see an impressive collection of coaches used by the imperial court, including the gilded coronation car of Karl VI.

ACROSS THE DANUBE

Prater Park

Over the Aspernbrücke, cross the Danube canal at the junction of Franz-Josefs-Kai and Stubenring. This takes you to **Prater Park**, an old-fashioned amusement park featuring roller-coasters, discos, shooting ranges, restaurants and beer halls. In the good old days, the Prater cafés were serenaded by the ubiquitous Strauss family and their archrival, Joseph Lanner.

If the Stephansdom had not already become the undisputed symbol of the city, the Prater's **Riesenrad** (giant Ferris wheel) would certainly have laid claim – especially after the famous ride of Orson Welles and Joseph Cotten in Carol Reed's film *The Third Man*. Built in 1897, by English engineer Walter B. Basset, it is one of the oldest and largest Ferris wheels in the world, 65m (213ft) high, and provides a great view over the city and the surrounding countryside. (The original wheel was built just five years earlier by American engineer George Ferris for the Columbian Fair in Chicago in 1893.)

Next to the Riesenrad is the terminal of the **Lilliputbahn** (Lilliputian Railway), which on summer weekends provides transport to the Fair Trade Grounds, the Planetarium and the Prater Museum.

The Riesenrad at the Prater

Donauinsel

You can reach the real Danube River (as opposed to the Danube Canal) along Lassallestrasse and over the Reichsbrücke. A man-made recreation island featuring beaches, barbecue picnic areas, and sports facilities, the **Donauinsel** runs 21km (13 miles) along the middle of the river.

You may be disappointed to discover that the 'Blue Danube' is actually yellowish brown in colour. This is due to the lime content of the riverbed. Be patient and continue on the Wagramerstrasse, past the attractive modern complex of buildings forming the UNO-City (officially Vienna International Centre, guided tours Mon–Fri 11am and 2pm) to the **Alte Donau** (the Old Danube). This self-contained arm of the river is closed off for sailing, fishing and bathing and is as blue as blue can

The soaring Millennium Tower

be. In the heart of the working-class 21st and 22nd districts, the banks are lined with beaches, marinas and neat gardens.

The **Donaupark** links the old and new Danube. More tranquil than the Prater, it has been laid out with flower beds, an artificial lake and sports arenas. It also features a chair lift and the 252-m (827-ft) tall **Donauturm** (Danube Tower), offering fine views from its terrace and revolving restaurant.

Back on the city side of the Danube, at Handelskai near the Nordbahnbrücke, is the **Millennium Tower**, completed in 1999. At over 200m (656ft), this is the highest enclosed building in Central Europe. It's an office and residential block and also houses Millennium City, a shopping, entertainment and leisure centre.

Leopoldsberg in the wine-growing district of Döbling

VIENNA'S SUBURBS

You should devote at least a day to exploring the 19th District of **Döbling**, the most gracious and elegant of Vienna's suburbs. Stretching from the Danube Canal to the slopes of the Wienerwald, Döbling includes Sievering, Grinzing, Heiligenstadt, Nussdorf and Kahlenberg. It is dotted with villas, parks, vineyards and, of course, the *Heuriger* wine gardens, which are especially popular in **Grinzing**.

Heiligenstadt and the other neighbourhoods of Döbling provide a vital clue to the secret of Vienna's charm. Vienna is not a conventional big city, but rather a collection of villages clustered around the Innere Stadt. These village-suburbs provide a convenient getaway from what the Viennese call the *Hektik* of metropolitan life.

If you do not have a car, start your tour by catching tram 37 in front of the Votivkirche at Schottentor, and take it to **Heiligenstadt**, the heart of Vienna's 'Beethoven country'.

You may want to stop off en route at the **Eroica House** (Döblinger Hauptstrasse 92; open Tues–Sun 9am–12.15pm and 1–4.30pm; admission fee), where Beethoven worked on his *Eroica* symphony during 1803–4, and at **Villa Wertheimstein** (Döblinger Hauptstrasse 96), a masterpiece of 19th-century Biedermeier architecture, full of period pieces, and featuring a lovely English garden.

At the end of the line (Heiligenstädter Park), walk across the park past the monument to Beethoven to Pfarrplatz 2, the prettiest of the composer's many Viennese homes. Take bus 38A to Probusgasse 6, the house where, in 1802, the composer penned his tragic *Heiligenstadt Testament*, in which he told his two brothers of his encroaching deafness. Today it is the **Beethoven Museum** (open Tues–Sun 9am–12.15pm and 1–4.30pm; admission fee).

Hohenstrasse

For a pleasant outing in the country, drive your car (or take the 38S bus from Grinzinger Allee) up to the **Höhenstrasse** leading to Kahlenberg and Leopoldsberg on the northern slopes of the Wienerwald. The route offers a grandiose view of the city

---

Singing in the Heuriger

The earliest Viennese song book was published in 1686, during the times of the legendary singer-songwriter Augustin Mitte. However, the flowering of song really took place in the 19th and early 20th centuries, when music became a part of the ambience of the *Heuriger* wine gardens. The songs are a curious blend of the comic and melancholic. Many of them are addressed to the city: '*Wien, Wien, nur du allein*' ('Vienna, Vienna, only you...') and '*Mei Mutterl war a Weanerin*' ('My Mother was Viennese...') are examples that still remain dear to the Viennese heart.

Klosterneuburg abbey

and surrounding country. You'll find it difficult to believe that you're still inside the city limits. If time permits, get out and walk around – the road has several inns and cafés where you can stop.

Since the end of the 18th century, the heights of **Kahlenberg** have been dotted with fashionable summer homes offering what is known as *Sommerfrische* (cool summer respite from the city heat). During two steaming hot days in July 1809, the Viennese aristocracy had a grandstand view of Napoleon's Battle of Wagram against the Austrians. Sipping cool Nussdorfer white wine, they watched the slaughter of 40,000 Austrians and 34,000 Frenchmen on the other side of the Danube.

The Höhenstrasse goes as far as **Leopoldsberg**, the very edge of the Wienerwald and the extreme eastern point of the European Alps. On a clear day, you can see about 100km (62 miles) eastwards from the terrace of the **Leopoldskirche** to the Carpathian Mountains of Slovakia.

Klosterneuberg

A short detour 7km (4 miles) to the north takes you to the imposing Augustine abbey of **Klosterneuburg**. A story claims it was founded by Duke Leopold III of Babenberg in 1106 on the spot where his bride's lost veil was discovered by his hunting dogs. In fact, its foundation is earlier, but little of the original edifice remains. Karl VI, who was very much taken with Spain, undertook expansive alterations in the 18th century, making it a baroque version of the Escorial. He wanted a combined palace and church with nine domes, each topped with a crown of the House of Habsburg. Only two were completed in his lifetime: the crown of the empire on the big dome and of the Austrian archduchy on the little one.

Klosterneuburg also features a museum of modern art, the **Sammlung Essl** (Essl Collection; open Tues–Sat 10am–7pm, Wed to 9pm; admission fee), a private foundation devoted to avant-garde Austrian artists and their representative American and European contemporaries.

The baroque ornamentation is indeed impressive, but the whole trip is made worthwhile by the **Leopoldskapelle**, with its magnificent **Verdun Altar** of 1181 containing 45 enamelled panels depicting scenes from the scriptures. It served as a graphic Bible for the poor who could not read the stories.

WIENERWALD

While it can be seen along the Höhenstrasse, to properly appreciate the **Wienerwald**, you must visit the villages hidden away in the forest to the south and southwest of Vienna.

Take Breitenfurterstrasse (behind Schönbrunn Palace) out to Perchtoldsdorf, a serene little village amid heather-covered hills, vineyards and fir trees. Continue south to Burg Liechtenstein, a 'ruined castle' built in 1873 on the site of the 12th-century home of the Liechtenstein dynasty. The park is an ideal spot for a picnic. In **Mödling** you can see the 15th-century Gothic Spitalkirche (church) and the house (Hauptstrasse 79) where Beethoven worked on his *Missa Solemnis*.

Turn west along route 11 to Hinterbrühl. Romantics like to believe that the picturesque mill, Höldrichsmühle (converted into an inn), is where Franz Schubert wrote songs for the miller's daughter Rosi (*'Die schöne Müllerin'*) in 1823. In fact the story originated in an 1864 operetta devoted to the composer's life. But the inn's wines can make believers of us all.

The road takes you to the Sattelbach Valley and the Cistercian abbey of **Heiligenkreuz** (Holy Cross), founded in 1133. Heiligenkreuz is named after the relic of a piece of the True Cross, given to Austria by the King of Jerusalem in the 12th century and kept in the tabernacle behind the high altar. The courtyard features a **Trinity Column** (Pillar of the Plague), the work of baroque artist Giovanni Giuliani, who also designed the basilica's splendid choir stalls. The structure retains its Romanesque western façade. Along its south side is a graceful 13th-century cloister with 300 red columns.

In the town **churchyard** you'll find a tomb bearing the inscription: *'Wie eine Blume sprosst der Mensch auf und wird gebrochen'* (*'Like a flower, the human being unfolds – and is broken'*). This is the grave of Mary Vetsera, the 17-year-old who died in 1889 at nearby **Mayerling** in a murder-suicide with Crown Prince Rudolf, heir to the Austro-Hungarian Empire. To hush the scandal-mongers, the hunting lodge where the Mayerling tragedy occurred was demolished shortly thereafter and replaced with a Carmelite convent.

Baden

Continue through the romantic Helenental Valley to the spa of **Baden,** 25km (16 miles) south of Vienna. Enjoyed by the Romans and made fashionable by Franz I in 1803, Baden became the very symbol of upright Viennese Biedermeier prosperity. The gentry of Vienna built their summer villas here and bathed in the 36°C (97°F) sulphurous waters. The thermal waters can still be enjoyed in the indoor pool (Brusattiplatz 4); open-air pools (Helenen Strasse 19–21); and mineral water pools (Marchetti Strasse 13). Return via **Gumpoldskirchen**, a village with first-rate *Heuriger* wine gardens.

DANUBE VALLEY

If your visit gives you time for only one side-trip it should
unquestionably be along the **Danube Valley**, in particular
the magical area known as the Wachau between the historic
towns of Melk and Krems.

Just an hour's drive west of Vienna, this is where the
Danube Valley is at its most scenic – in turn both charming
and smiling with vineyards, apricot orchards and rustic villages, then suddenly forbidding with ruined medieval castles
and rocky cliffs half hidden in mist.

You cannot wax too romantic in describing the scenery,
for this is a landscape whose atmosphere is heavy with myth.
Legend has it that the Burgundy kings of the medieval German epic, the *Nibelungenlied,* passed this spot en route to the
kingdom of the Huns. The crusaders also passed through

The ruined 13th-century Burg Aggstein

High above the Danube, the clifftop Benedictine abbey of Melk

here on their way to the Holy Land. Take the Danube River steamer if you simply want to sit and dream as this mythical world passes you by. For a closer look at the towns and castles on the way it's best to travel around by car.

Melk

On a leisurely tour of the Danube Valley, 84km (52 miles) by the Westautobahn from Vienna, the Benedictine abbey of **Melk** *(Stift Melk)* makes an ideal starting point. Towering high above the river on a protruding rock, this is one of the region's most majestic sights. Its position overlooking a bend in the river made this a strategic site from the time of the Romans. The Babenberg predecessors of the Habsburgs had a palace stronghold here in the 10th century, which they handed over to the Benedictines in 1106. The monks gradually created an abbey of huge proportions, enhanced by the baroque transformations of architect Jakob Prandtauer in 1702.

Two towers, together with the octagonal dome and the lower Bibliothek (Library) and Marmorsaal (Marble Hall), form a harmonious group. The interior of the church is rich in reds and golds with a high altar by Antonio Beduzzi and superbly sculpted pulpit, choir and confessionals. The ceiling frescoes are by Johann Michael Rottmayr, whose work also adorns Vienna's Karlskirche.

Before crossing the River Danube, make a quick detour to the village of **Mauer**, 10km (6 miles) due east of Melk, to see the late-Gothic wooden altarpiece in the parish church. The work, by an anonymous local artist around 1515, depicts the *Adoration of the Virgin Mary* with a wealth of vivid detail.

Medieval Towns of the Wachau

The Wachauer Strasse, along the north bank, is dotted with apricot orchards and vineyards, 18th-century *Weinhüterhütten* (vine-guard's huts) and villages with *Heuriger* wine gardens.

On the opposite bank, you can see Schönbühel and the 13th-century ruins of **Burg Aggstein**. The castle was once owned by a robber baron named Jörg Scheck vom Wald, popularly known as 'Schreckenwald' (Terror of the Forest). One of his favourite activities was to lead prisoners to his rose garden, on the edge of a sheer precipice, where they were given the choice of either starving to death or ending it quickly by jumping 53m (175ft) onto the rocks below.

Back on the happier north bank, visit the town of **Spitz**, with its late-Gothic **St Mauritius** church. It's known for its statues of the apostles in the 1380 organ gallery, and the baroque painting of the *Martyrdom of St Mauritius* by Kremser (Martin Johann) Schmidt. In the village of **St Michael**, look for seven stone hares perched on the roof of the 16th-century church. These commemorate a particularly vicious winter when snowdrifts were said to have enabled the animals to jump clear over the church. In the village of

Dürnstein's abbey church

Weissenkirchen is a fortified church, which was originally surrounded by four towers, a moat, ramparts and 44 cannons to fend off the Turks.

The most romantic of these medieval towns is **Dürnstein**, famous as the site of Richard the Lion Heart's imprisonment in 1192–3 *(see opposite)*. Devastated by the Swedish army in 1645, the castle of Kuenringer is more interesting to look at from below than it is to visit. But do make a point of seeing Dürnstein's **abbey church**, a baroque structure with a splendid carved wooden door to the abbey courtyard and an imposing statue of the resurrected Christ at the church entrance.

Krems

Your journey through the Wachau will end delightfully with a visit to **Krems**, heart of the region's wine industry and historically one of the Danube Valley's most important trading centres. Today, you can enjoy its superb Gothic, Renaissance and baroque residences on tranquil, tree-shaded squares.

Park on Südtiroler Platz and walk through the 15th-century Steiner Tor (town gate) with its Gothic pepper pot towers. Turn left up Schmidgasse to Körnermarkt and the Dominikanerkirche (Dominican church), transformed into an important museum of medieval art. Continue round to Pfarrplatz, dominated by the **Pfarrkirche**, a lovely church remodelled (1616–30) by two Italian architects and decorated with altar paintings by Franz Anton Maulbertsch and the masterful frescoes of Kremser Schmidt. The oldest square in Krems, Hoher Markt, features a masterpiece of Gothic residential architecture, the arcaded **Gozzoburg**, built around 1270. Take a stroll along the Untere Landstrasse to see some elegant baroque façades and the fine Renaissance **Rathaus** (town hall).

On a contemporary note, a cartoon museum has opened in the town, the **Karikaturmuseum** (Steiner Landstrasse 3a; <www.karikaturmuseum.at>). Its roof architecture is inspired by Alpine peaks, though the mountains wear a pointed hat, and two windows and a red light make a face on the front of the building. It includes work by the Austrian cartoonist Manfred Deix, who was renowned for being less than flattering to his fellow-countrymen.

Before leaving Krems, treat yourself to the local 'new wine' served in one of the leafy arcaded courtyards along the Obere Landstrasse. Then let somebody else chauffeur you back to Vienna (90km/56 miles on route S3).

A Song for Richard

During the Crusade of 1191, the brave but cheeky English king, Richard the Lion Heart, enraged Leopold V von Babenberg by replacing the Austrian flag in Acre, Palestine, with the English one. Worse than that, he prevented the Austrians from sharing in the booty. But, on his way home, though dressed as a peasant, Richard was recognised and thrown into the darkest dungeon of Dürnstein. He languished there for several years until the faithful minstrel Blondel came looking for him, singing a song known only to the king and himself. Richard revealed his place of imprisonment by joining in the chorus. His ransom, 23,000kg (22.6 tons), of silver, was enough to finance the Holy Roman Empire's expedition to Sicily and to build a new Ring Wall around Vienna.

TO THE EAST

The Bratislava road east from Vienna (route 9) follows the Danube and traces the ancient Eastern European boundary of the Roman Empire. Just 36km (22 miles) along, are the remains of **Carnuntum**. Once the capital of the Roman province of Pannonia (embracing much of modern Hungary and eastern Austria), it has now been absorbed by the town of Petronell. In the second century, under Hadrian and Marcus Aurelius, Carnuntum was a thriving commercial centre. On the right before you reach the town is the amphitheatre, where a summer festival is held.

From Petronell drive 5km (3 miles) south to **Rohrau**, the birthplace of Joseph Haydn. You can visit the beautifully restored thatched farmhouse where he was born in 1732. Concerts are held here during spring and summer. Nearby is the Schloss Rohrau, the baroque castle of the Harrach family, early patrons of young Haydn. The castle has a fine collection of 17th-century Spanish, Flemish and Italian art.

Continue on to **Neusiedler See**. This birdwatchers' paradise teems with heron, teal, waterfowl, wild geese and egret. The water of the lake is so shallow that it's possible to wade right across – only a few spots are more than 1.5m (5ft) deep. If you do cross make sure you're armed with your passport and a visa for your arrival on the other side – the southern end of the lake belongs to Hungary. Flat-bottomed boats can be hired for fishing. In winter you can go skating and ice-sailing; in summer operettas are performed on the landing stages.

Along the lake's western shores are the villages of **Rust** and **Mörbisch**. Both are famous for the storks that favour their chimneys for nesting. In Mörbisch, on the Hungarian border, walk along the shady lanes, with their spotless whitewashed houses colourfully decorated with flowers and bouquets of maize. The wine gardens here are truly idyllic.

The baroque town of **Eisenstadt**, 52km (32 miles) south of the city, is where Joseph Haydn worked from 1761 as musical director for the Hungarian prince, Paul Esterhazy. His house, the **Haydn Museum** (Joseph Haydn Gasse 21; open Apr–Oct daily 9am–5pm; admission fee) contains his collection of paintings, sheets of music and personal possessions. Haydn loved Eisenstadt and wanted to live and die here. He managed the living, but died in Vienna, without having taken the precaution of specifying where he wanted to be buried. Unfortunately, shortly after he was buried in Vienna in 1809, someone stole his skull, which was put on exhibition. The headless body was eventually returned to Eisenstadt where the skull rejoined it in 1954. He is now in a white marble grave at the **Bergenkirche**. The church is also noted for a Kalvarienberg, a Calvary display of life size figures showing the stations of the cross, displayed in a series of austere dungeon-like rooms.

Fisherman at Neusiedler See

WHAT TO DO

ENTERTAINMENT

Opera

Its difficult to think of a cultural institution in another European capital that holds the privileged place of the **Staatsoper** (State Opera, <www.weiner-staatsoper.at>) in Vienna. Since this is Austria, even people who loathe opera (never having seen one) can be tempted in and converted. Try to make Mozart your first opera; after that you'll be ready to take on Wagner and even Alban Berg.

If you have tickets for a premiere or other gala performance, you should wear evening dress, though even on an ordinary night, people turn up in black tie or long dress.

First-rate opera can also be heard at the **Volksoper** (Währingerstrasse 78), and operetta and ballet at the **Theater an der Wien** (Linke Wienzeile 6).

Music

Music is an integral part of Vienna. There really is something for everyone, with concerts at the historic palaces, including Schönbrunn and the Belvedere, **Musikverein** (Dumbastrasse 3 <www.musikverein.at>), **Konzerthaus** (Lothringestrasse 20 <www.konzerthaus.at>), and the **Staatsoper** (<www.wiener-staatsoper.at>). Festivals take place throughout the year.

It is easy to find operas and operettas, chamber music, traditional singing, jazz and, of course, there are many opportunities to hear the music of composers associated with the city. In fact, the music of Mozart, Haydn, Schubert and Beethoven is performed in Vienna's oldest concert hall, the **Mozarthaus** (Singerstrasse 7, <www.mozarthaus.at>). You should also try to hear the celebrated **Wiener Sängerknaben** (Vienna Boys' Choir), who sing at Sunday Mass and other festivities in the Burgkapelle in the Hofburg *(see page 45)*.

Music in Vienna is not only in the classical tradition. The joyful sounds of Strauss waltzes can still be heard at concerts in the Stadtpark, in the Prater cafés and in the Wienerwald *Heuriger* (wine gardens).

Theatre

The **Burgtheater** (National Theatre; Dr Karl Lueger Ring 2) is not just Vienna's proudest theatre, but also one of the leading ensembles of the German-speaking world. The **Akademietheater** (Lisztrasse 1) focuses on modern and avant-garde drama. Performances are held all year round at Vienna's **English Theatre** at Josefsgasse 12. There are several English-speaking theatre groups in the city and

The Burgtheater is renowned for its thought-provoking productions

special performances are
staged for children.

Nightlife

The city is said to have more
than 6,000 bars, nightclubs,
discos and cabarets – with
many of the most popular

Clubs come and go so
consult a copy of
Partytimer, the weekly
listings magazine, for
the latest information
about nightclubs,
parties and lounges.

bars staying open round the clock. There are a few large
clubs, but also many small venues with music provided by
well-known DJs. There are cool lounge clubs, too, where
people chill to easy-listening sounds.

North of Stephansdom, the area around Ruprechtsplatz,
Seitenstettengasse and Rabensteig forms what is known as
the **Bermudadreieck** (Bermuda Triangle), where people go
to drop out of sight of more conventional establishments.
Names change with each new owner, but the bars remain
full. More chic is the district around **Bäckerstrasse**, with the
long-established bar and restaurant, Oswald & Kalb, at its
centre. The nightclubs around **Kärntnerstrasse** cater (at a
price) to the tourist trade. People with more traditional tastes
enjoy the sentimental violin and zither music of the Balkan
restaurants, the Schrammelmusik (violin, guitar and accor-
dion trios) of the *Heuriger* wine gardens *(see page 94)*, and
the oom-pah-pah brass band of the Prater.

SPORTS

With a foresight that nobody gives them credit for, the Habsburgs provided modern **joggers** with the perfect route,
which doesn't require them even to leave the Innere Stadt.
Start at the Burgtheater end of the Volksgarten near the monument to Empress Elisabeth, trot past the Theseus Temple,
once around the duck pond to the statue of dramatist Franz
Grillparzer, and then across Heldenplatz past Archduke Karl

and Prince Eugene. Skirt the edge of the Neue Hofburg and whip around the Burggarten to salute the monuments to Goethe and Mozart. The entire route from Sissi to Wolfgang Amadeus and back shouldn't take more than 30 minutes.

Cycling and **in-line skating** are enjoyable ways of getting around Vienna – and of escaping traffic snarls. Bicycles can be rented from any one of 160 Austrian railway stations. In Vienna, the three stations that rent bicycles are Westbahnhof, Wien Nord and Floridsdorf. You can return your bicycle to any participating Austrian railway station. The free *See Vienna by Bike* brochure from the tourist information office lists bicycle hire firms, and also provides regional maps of cycling routes. The Prater has an in-line skate rental outlet near the Riesenrad Ferris wheel (tel: 597 8288). (You will need some form of ID card to rent a bike.)

See Vienna's spectacular hinterland by **hiking** along the well-marked paths of the Wienerwald. In the winter, these paths can be used for **cross-country skiing**.

The 21-km (13-mile) beach of the Donauinsel *(see page 68)* provides outdoor **swimming**, along with facilities for **waterskiing** and **windsurfing**. Döbling's Krapfenwaldlbad is a fashionable outdoor swimming pool, complete with champagne bar. Most handsome of the indoor swimming pools is the Amalienbad, Reumannplatz 23, with *Jugendstil* decor and an old-fashioned steambath and sauna.

Tennis and **squash** players will find dozens of courts in the Prater at Rustenschacher Allee and in the Donaupark, Kratochwjlestrasse and Eiswerkstrasse. There is a huge **bowling** alley in the Prater (Hauptallee 124). The Freudenau area of the Prater has an 18-hole **golf** course, **horse racing**, **horse riding** and **polo**. You can see professional football in the Prater, home of the town's first division team, Austria.

Ice-skating carries on year round in the Wiener Stadthalle, Vogelweidplatz 14.

SHOPPING

Not surprisingly the most important shopping attraction in Vienna, a town preoccupied by its history, is **antiques**. Furniture and *objets d'art* from all over the old empire have ended up here in the little shops in the Innere Stadt around the Josefsplatz: in Augustinerstrasse, Spiegelgasse, Plankengasse and Dorotheergasse. You can still find authentic rococo, Biedermeier and *Jugendstil* pieces, including signed furniture by the great designers Michael Thonet and Josef Hoffmann.

Your best chance of finding a bargain is in the auction rooms of the **Dorotheum** (Dorotheergasse 17). This state pawnshop, popularly known as 'Tante Dorothee', was set up by Emperor Joseph I to enable the *nouveaux pauvres* to realise a quick return on heirlooms. But it was also a kind of state-sponsored clearing house for stolen art objects, where the original owners could even buy their property back if the police had not managed to catch the thieves. Items are put on display before the sale, often in the windows of a bank opposite the auction rooms. If you feel uncertain about bidding, you can hire a licensed agent to do it for you for a small fee.

Still in the realm of the past are the speciality shops

Braun on the Graben

for **coin-** and **stamp-collectors** (where else could you expect to find mint-condition Bosnia-Herzegovina issues of 1914?).

The **Augarten porcelain** workshops turn out hand-decorated rococo chinaware, including figures of the Lipizzaner horses. **Petit-point embroidery** is available in the form of handbags, cushions and other items with flower, folk and opera motifs. Viennese craftsmen are also noted for their ceramics, dolls, enamel miniatures and costume jewellery.

You will find the more elegant shops on the Kärntnerstrasse, Graben and Kohlmarkt. Traditional Austrian costume *(Trachten)* has caught the whimsical attention of high fashion with the **Dirndl**, a pleated skirt with a blue- or pink-and-white apron tied at the waist and a white full-sleeved blouse under a laced bodice. For men the heavy woollen **Loden** cloth makes excellent winter coats.

The Saturday morning **flea market** on the Naschmarkt is a veritable Aladdin's Cave.

CHILDREN'S ACTIVITIES

Vienna provides a wide range of attractions for children. In the interactive museum at **Schönbrunn** *(see page 64)* they delight in discovering how the Habsburgs lived. The **Marionette Theatre** and maze offer more enchantments and there's a cellar devoted to the baking and tasting of *strudel*. There's a **zoo** at Schönbrunn and a **vivarium** at Esterhazy Park, with sharks, piranhas and snakes. For gentler souls, there's the **Butterfly House** at Burggarten, and for those

A passion for flowers

who like stars, the **Planetarium** (Oswald Thomas Platz <www.planetarium-wien.at>). At the **Hofburg** palace *(see page 40)*, one can learn all about Empress Sissi, her clothes, hairstyling, horse-riding and beauty recipes.

Among the most interesting museums for children is **Zoom Kindermuseum** *(see page 52;* advance booking, tel: 524 79 08; <www.kindermuseum.at>). The **Museum of Modern Art Ludwig Foundation, Museum of Fine Arts** and **Museum of Natural History** all have children's programmes. The **Museum of Technology** has interactive exhibits <www.technischesmuseum.at>. At the **House of Music** (Seilerstatte 30; open 10am–10pm; <www.hdm.at>) you can feel, hear, see and play music and mix CDs.

Kids at Schönbrunn

The fair at the **Prater**, the **Spanish Riding School** *(see page 42)* and the view from the **Donauturm** *(see page 69)* are all must-sees. Playgrounds and beaches can be found on **Danube Island**. In summer, the **boats** on the Danube sometimes sail with conjurers and jugglers, and offer special tours of the captain's bridge <www.ddsg-blue-danube.at>. At Christmas, a skating rink appears outside City Hall.

For more information about events for youngsters, contact Babenbergerstrasse 1, Mon–Sat noon–7pm, tel: 1799 (4000-84 088) <www.jugendinfowien.at>.

Calendar of Events

For information and ticket details, contact the Tourist Information Office, tel: 2111 4222, or consult <www.info.wien.at>.

January Vienna Philharmonic's traditional *Neujahrskonzert* (New Year's Day concert), 11am, at Musikverein; jazz-lovers' alternative: Vienna Art Orchestra, 9pm, at Sofiensäle, Marxergasse 17.

February/March *Opernball* (Opera Ball), at Staatsoper, the social event of the year; the *Ball der Philharmoniker* (Philharmonic Ball), at Musikverein, rivals the *Opernball* for prestige; *Fasching* (Carnival) procession in Döbling.

April *Ostermarkt* (Easter Market): a country-fair atmosphere on Freyung in Innere Stadt; *Wiener Sängerknaben* (Vienna Boys' Choir) weekly Mass in the Hofburg's Burgkapelle; *OsterKlang Wien* (Vienna's Sounds of Easter) music festival.

May Traditional May Day celebrations at Prater amusement park; Vienna Marathon accompanied by popular festivities; the Life Ball, an AIDS charity event supported by international celebrities.

June *Wiener Festwochen* (Vienna Festival) featuring music, dance and theatrical productions at Theater an der Wien and Messepalast; Regenbogen (Gay Rainbow) Parade on Ringstrasse; *Donaueninselfest* (Danube Island Festival) with funfair festivities.

July/August *Jazzfest Wien* (Vienna Jazz Festival) at Staatsoper and Burgtheater; Donauinsel pop music festival, a free weekend event; *Wiener Musiksommer*, summer festival of popular opera and operetta at Theater an der Wien; *Klangbogen* musical recitals in palaces and outdoors; jazz, rock, reggae and hip-hop music festival at Wiesen, south of Vienna.

September Schönbrunn Palace festival; In-line Skating Marathon on the Ringstrasse.

October Viennale Film Festival; *Wean Hean* folk festival.

November/December *Christkindlmarkt* (Christmas Market) at Rathausplatz, Schönbrunn, Freyung, Spittelberg: carols, roast chestnuts, *Gluhwein* and stalls laden with gifts; MuseumsQuartier courtyard decked with lights and decorations; concerts, recitals throughout the Innere Stadt; New Year's Eve *Kaiserball* (Emperor's Ball) opens the ball season in Hofburg.

EATING OUT

When it comes to Viennese cuisine, it is worth bearing in mind that this city was once the centre of the old Habsburg Empire of 60 million Eastern and Southern Europeans. The emperor and his archdukes and generals have gone, but not the Bohemian dumplings, the Hungarian goulash, the Polish stuffed cabbage and Serbian *shashlik*, and the plum, cherry and apricot brandies that accompany the Turkish coffee. And all are now frequently served with the lighter touch of the New Viennese Cuisine.

Sautéed to perfection, Wiener Schnitzel as served at Figlmüller

VIENNESE FARE

Two Viennese staples that you're likely to come across immediately are the *Wiener Schnitzel* and the *Backhendl*. The *Wiener Schnitzel* is a large, thinly sliced cutlet of veal crisply sautéed in a coating of egg and seasoned breadcrumbs. *Backhendl* is roast chicken prepared in the same way. Viennese gourmets insist that the *Wiener Schnitzel* be served with cold potato or cucumber salad. You should also make sure that it is a cut of veal *(vom Kalb)* and not pork *(vom Schwein)*, as in some of the cheaper establishments. The *Backhendl* is sometimes served with *Geröstete* (sautéed potatoes).

Tafelspitz (boiled beef) was Emperor Franz Joseph's favourite dish, and to this day is a form of ambrosia to the Viennese. Spice it up with *Kren* (horseradish) and *Schnitt-lauchsauce* (chive sauce). Another delight, originally from Hungary, is goulash – beef chunks stewed in onions, garlic, paprika, tomatoes and celery. *Debreziner* sausages, *Kömény-magleves Nokedival* (caraway-seed soup with dumplings) and apple soup are three more Hungarian specialities.

From the Czech Republic comes Prague ham and *sauer-kraut* soup; from Polish Galicia, roast goose; and from Ser-bia, peppery barbecued *cevapcici* meatballs and *schaschlik* brochettes of lamb with onions and green and red peppers.

Dumplings *(Knödel),* made from flour, yeast, or potatoes, are an Austrian staple. The *Marillenknödel* is a dessert dumpling, made of potato with a piping hot apricot inside. Another delicious dessert dumpling is the *Topfenknödel,* made with a cream-cheese filling.

Hot desserts are, in fact, a speciality and you should also try *Buchteln* or *Wuchteln*, yeast buns often filled with plum jam, and from Hungary the *Palatschinken,* pancakes filled

---

Viennese Sausage Stands

They all go for it: society ladies in posh frocks, night owls, opera buffs, workers – they all stand together at the Sausage Stand. Typical fare includes frankfurters (usual hot dog sausage), *Debreziner* (thin and spicy), *Bratwurst* (hunky thick fried sausage) and *Kasekrainer* (thick and made with meat and cheese). *Burenwurst* is a sort of boiled *Bratwurst*. There are stands all over town, but to get you started: Albertina Wurstelstand, Augustinerplatz, 8am–4am; Hoher Markt, Marc Aurel Strasse, 7am–4am; Zur Oper, Kärntnerstrasse 10am–5am.

Viennese wine is best sipped alfresco in a *Heuriger* garden

with jam or nuts. And don't forget the *Apfelstrudel*, a flaky pastry filled with thinly sliced apples, raisins and cinnamon.

Finally, there's the most famous and sinfully delicious chocolate cake in the world, the *Sachertorte*. Join in the endless debate over whether or not it should be split into two layers and where the apricot jam should go.

Wines and Wine Gardens

Wine in Vienna is almost always white, which the Viennese drink with meat and fish alike. The best known of Austrian white wines, the *Gumpoldskirchner*, has the full body and bouquet of its southern vineyards. The Viennese give equal favour to their own *Grinzinger, Nussdorfer, Sieveringer* and *Neustifter*. From the Danube Valley, with an extra natural sparkle, come the *Kremser, Dürnsteiner* and *Langenloiser*.

Of the reds, the *Vöslauer*, produced in Bad Vöslau near Baden, and the *Kalterersee*, imported from South Tyrol (now

Alto Adige in Italy), are about the best. *Blaufränkisch* and *Zweigelt* are also reliable standbys. To enjoy these wines in their original state, they should be ordered *herb* (dry). Often the producers will sweeten them for the foreign palate unless you specify otherwise. Perhaps the most pleasant thing about Viennese wine is the way in which it is drunk.

The Viennese have created a splendid institution, the *Heuriger*, where you can sip white wine on mild evenings under the stars. Winemakers are allowed by law to sell a certain amount of their new wine (also called *Heuriger*) directly to the public. They announce the new wine by hanging out a sprig of pine over the door and a sign saying *Ausg'steckt* (open). The *Heuriger* of Grinzing are extremely popular, but many of the best ones are out in Nussdorf, Ober-Sievering and Neustift. *Heuriger* gardens are generally open from mid-afternoon until late in the evening and at weekends for lunch. The season runs from March to October.

The local *Gösser* beer presents a fair challenge to the powerful *Pilsner Urquell* imported from the Czech Republic. Among the brandies you should try the Hungarian *Barack* (apricot) and Serbian *Slivovitz* (plum).

Chocolate-rich Sachertorte

Coffee and the Kaffeehaus

The varieties of coffee in Vienna are virtually endless, and there are names for every shade from black to white. Ask for *einen kleinen Mokka* and you'll get a small, strong black coffee and stamp yourself as someone of French or Italian taste. A *Kapuziner*, topped with generous dollops

Passing the time of day in the plush Café Diglas

of cream, is more Viennese; *ein Brauner*, with just a dash of milk, is as Viennese as can be. *Eine Melange* (pronounced 'melanksch'), a mixture of milk and coffee, is designed for sensitive stomachs; *ein Einspänner*, with whipped cream in a tall glass, is for aunts on Sundays; *ein Türkischer*, prepared semisweet in a copper pot, is for addicts of the Balkan Connection.

The Viennese *Kaffeehaus* dates back to the 17th century when, depending on which legend you choose, either a Polish spy named Kulczycki or a Greek merchant named Theodat opened the first café with a stock of coffee beans captured from the Turks. By the time of Maria Theresa the town was full of coffee houses, fashionable and shady, where gentry and intellectuals mingled. Some developed their own particular clientele – writers, artists, politicians – while the most prominent (Griensteidl, Café Central, Herrenhof) attracted all types.

After a post-war lull, the institution made a grand comeback. In the Innere Stadt, the renovated Café Central and the

Coffee-house confection

more sedate Griensteidl are thriving once again. Café Hawelka, at Dorotheergasse 6, once popular with artists and antiques dealers, has become a hangout for the younger crowd. Artists now prefer Alt-Wien, at Bäckerstrasse 9, and the Kleines Café, Franziskanerplatz 3, with its superb interior design by architect Hermann Czech. Intellectuals have followed the example of the late Thomas Bernhard in favouring Café Bräunerhof, at Stallburggasse 2. This café is also popular with music-lovers for its weekend chamber-music recitals. Chess players with a killer instinct can be seen at the Café Museum, Friedrichstrasse 6. In the Sixth District, Café Sperl, Gumpendorfer Strasse 11, is an elegant 100-year-old establishment with marble tables, *Jugendstil* chairs, an endless row of newspapers (including *The Times*, *Le Monde* and *La Stampa*), and billiard tables for those who really can't bear to sit and do nothing.

Help with a Viennese Menu

Apfelstrudel	pastry with apples, raisins and cinnamon
Auflauf	soufflé or casserole
Backhendl	chicken sautéed in egg and breadcrumbs
Bauernschmaus	meat with dumplings and sauerkraut
Beuschel	chopped offal in sauce

Blunzn	black pudding
Buchteln/Wuchteln	yeast buns filled with plum jam
Debreziner	spicy Hungarian sausage
Eierschwammerl	mushrooms
Faschiertes	minced meat
Fleischlaberl	meat rissoles
Frittatensuppe	broth with sliced crêpes
Gefüllte Paprika	stuffed green pepper
Germknödel	yeast dumpling
Griessnockerlsuppe	semolina dumpling soup
Guglhupf	Viennese cake
Kaiserschmarrn	pancake served with fruit compote
Kalbsvögerl	knuckle of veal
Knödel	flour, potato or yeast dumplings
Krenfleisch	boiled pork served with horseradish
Marillenknödel	apricot dumpling
Millirahmstrudel	strudel with sweet cheese filling
Nockerl	small dumpling
Palatschinken	pancakes filled with jam or nuts
Paradeiser	tomatoes
Powidl	plum sauce
Ribisel	red or black currants
Rostbraten	pot roast
Rotkraut	red cabbage
Sachertorte	chocolate cake
Schinkenfleckerl	baked noodles with chopped ham
Schwammerlsuppe	mushroom soup
Tafelspitz	boiled beef
Topfenknödel	dumpling with a cream-cheese filling
Topfenstrudel	strudel with cream cheese and raisins
Wiener Schnitzel	veal or pork fillet fried in breadcrumbs
Zigeunerschnitzel	Wiener Schnitzel with paprika
Zwetschkenröster	plum compote
Zwiebelrostbraten	beef steak with fried onions

HANDY TRAVEL TIPS

An A–Z Summary of Practical Information

A

ACCOMMODATION (For RECOMMENDED HOTELS, see page 125)

The Vienna Tourist Board publishes a list of hotels, *Pensionen* (guest houses) and *Saison-Hotels* (student hostels used as hotels from July to September) with details about amenities, prices and classifications. You can pick it up, along with an excellent free city map, from the Austrian Tourist Board in your country or from travel agents. Tourist information offices in Vienna *(see page 122)* can book rooms for you, for a small fee. Telephone assistance is available year-round through Wien-Hotels, tel: 43 124 555; fax: 43 124 555 666; or log on to the Tourist Board's website <www.info. wien.at>. If you do cancel your reservation, the hotel has a right to charge a cancellation fee.

The friendly atmosphere of a pension in Vienna makes it popular for longer stays, though, as with some of the cheaper hotels, not all of them have rooms with private baths. Apartments are also available for longer stays. It is always advisable to book ahead, especially for travel from Easter to the end of September, and at Christmas and New Year. It is also possible to stay in private homes on a bed-and-breakfast basis. This is an especially attractive option in some of the smaller villages around Vienna. The famous old luxury hotels around the Opera are often fully booked by a long-established clientele, so reservations are necessary well in advance. However 'old fashioned' they may appear on the outside, Vienna's luxury hotels often have full, state-of-the-art business, sports and fitness facilities.

a guest house	**eine Pension**
a single/double room	**ein Einzel-/Doppelzimmer**
with/without bath (shower)	**mit/ohne Bad (Dusche)**
What's the rate per night?	**Was kostet eine Übernachtung?**

AIRPORT *(Flughafen)*

Wien-Schwechat Airport <live.viennaairport.com>, about 20km
(12 miles) from the centre of Vienna, handles domestic and international flights. The modern terminal has a bank, restaurants, cafés,
news and souvenir stands, a duty-free shop and the Vienna Airport
Tourist Information Office. The City Airport Train (CAT), which
leaves every 30 minutes, provides a high-speed (16 minutes) connection to the City Air Terminal at Landstrasse (Wien Mitte). There
is also the Schnellbahn (S-Bahn), which takes longer but is much
cheaper. Airport shuttle buses leave every 30 minutes for Schwedenplatz or UNO-City. The Mazur Airport Service is a private shuttle service that takes you to your exact address, tel: 7007 32901.

B

BICYCLE AND IN-LINE SKATE RENTALS

(Fahrrad/In-Line-Skater-Verleih)

With the increase in bicycle lanes, both cycling and in-line skating
are growing in popularity among tourists as well as local citizens as
a way of beating the traffic snarls. The Ringstrasse makes a perfect
circular route for seeing the sights, and the Wienerwald on the city
outskirts has 230km (144 miles) of cycle paths through the
woods – for leisurely family excursions or mountain-bikers.
Bicycles are available to rent from bike hire shops and at main-line
railway stations. Pedal Power <www.pedalpower.at> hires out
bikes and organises guided tours (advance booking required).

BUDGETING FOR YOUR TRIP

To give you an idea of what to expect, here is a list of average
prices in euros (€). They can only be approximate, however, as in
Austria, too, inflation creeps relentlessly up.

One way to save money is the Vienna Card *(see opposite)*, available from the Tourist Information Office *(see page 123)*. It provides

discounts on transport, sightseeing, shopping and entertainment.

Airport. City Airport Train (CAT) to city centre €8 single, €15 return; S-Bahn €3.

Bicycle rental. Adult €27, child €19, student €21 for one day.

Car rental. (advance booking from abroad) from €70 per day, from €250 for three days.

Entertainment. Cinema from €8, nightclub from about €40, disco from about €5.

Guides. From €100 for half a day.

Hotels. (double room with bath or shower per night, including breakfast). ***** €180–720, **** €96–240, *** €65–190, ** €43–143, * €62–80 *(see Recommended Hotels, page 125)*.

Meals. The average cost of a standard meal, including a glass of wine is between €18 and €25 per person.

Museums. Entrance fees vary considerably. Concessions are available at many museums for holders of the Vienna Card *(see below)*. Entrance for children under six is free. There is a reduction for schoolchildren (passport required) and students (international student identity card required).

Public transport. €1.50 for single ticket, €5 for a 24-hour ticket, €12 for a 72-hour ticket. Children under six years old travel free. Children under 15 are allowed to travel free on Sundays and public holidays and during the Viennese school holidays on presentation of an identity card.

Sightseeing. *Fiaker:* about €30 for a short tour and €60 for a longer one (although not all that much longer); *MS Vindobona* motorboat: from about €10.

Taxis. Meter starts at €2, €1 per km or €0.20 per minute.

Tickets. Concerts €5–€55; opera €5–€185; Spanish Riding School morning training, adults €11.50, senior citizens €8.50, children €5; performances, €33–€145 <www.spanische-reitschule.com>; Vienna Boys' Choir €5–€20 <www.wsk.at>.

Vienna Card. The Vienna Card provides reduced admission and other benefits at 180 museums and sights, theatres, concert halls, shops, restaurants, cafés and wine gardens *(Heuriger)*; unlimited travel by underground, bus and tram, and a reduction on the shuttle bus to/from the city centre.

The card costs €16.90 and is valid for 72 hours. It can be purchased at Vienna Airport and at hotels and tourist information offices, and by credit card, tel: 43 1 798 44 00-148.

C

CAMPING

For information about campsites, camping and caravanning <www. campsite.at> is helpful if you can read German. Of camping sites located around the city, one is open all year: Wien West I/II, Hüttel-bergstrasse 40 and 80, tel: 43 1 941 449 or 43 1 942 314. Other sites: Aktiv Camping Neue Donau, Am Kleehäufel, tel: 43 1 202 4010 (mid-May–Sept); Wien Süd, An der Au 2, tel: 43 1 888 4154 (July–Aug).

CAR RENTAL/HIRE *(Autovermietung)* (See also DRIVING)

For travelling inside the city, parking would make a car more of a hindrance than an asset, but having a car is certainly useful for excursions out to the Wienerwald and the Danube Valley.

Though some local firms may offer lower prices than Avis, Budget, Europcar and Hertz, these international agencies are more likely to let you return the car elsewhere in the country at no extra cost. The best deal can usually be obtained through your travel agency before leaving home.

Third-party insurance is compulsory, but full cover is recommended. To avoid unpleasant surprises, make sure the price quoted includes all the necessary insurance and taxes.

To hire a car, you must show your driving licence (held for at least a year) and passport. You also need a major credit card, or a large deposit will be required. The minimum age for renting cars ranges from 20 to 23.

Avis, tel: 43 1 7007 32700, 32961 <www.avis.co.uk>

Budget, tel: 43 1 7007 32711, 33659 <www.budget.co.uk>

Denzeldrive, tel: 0800 0800 800 (toll free; <www.denzeldrive.at>) has special deals for Vienna Card holders.

Europcar, tel: 43 1 7007 333 16 <www.europcar.co.uk>

Hertz, tel: 43 1 7007 32661, 32432 <www.hertz.co.uk>

I'd like to rent a car (for today). **Ich möchte (für heute) ein Auto mieten.**

CLIMATE

Spring is Vienna's most pleasant season. Chestnut trees and white lilacs are in blossom for the city's music festival. In July and August the Viennese leave the city relatively free for visitors, and in autumn, the Wienerwald is in splendid colour for the *Heuriger* wine gardens, and the opera and theatre season in the city centre. Even in winter Vienna is worth the trip for a marvellous white Christmas, despite of the cold east wind.

The chart shows Vienna's average monthly temperatures:

	J	F	M	A	M	J	J	A	S	O	N	D
°F	30	34	41	50	59	64	68	66	61	50	41	34
°C	-1	1	5	10	15	18	20	19	16	10	5	1

CLOTHING *(Kleidung)*

For the extremes of Vienna's weather, take light cottons for the very hot summer afternoons and your warmest woollens for the bitter winter. That wind off the steppes can whip through at any time; so even in summer, for an occasional cool evening, take a sweater and raincoat. The Viennese like to dress up for the theatre, concerts and opera, but a dark suit or cocktail dress is nearly always appropriate. A dinner jacket (tuxedo) or evening dress may be worn on special occasions, such as for premieres and galas.

COMPLAINTS *(Reklamationen)*

Modern Vienna is remarkably efficient, but if something should go wrong, report the matter to the Vienna Tourist Board *(see page 123)*. In hotels, restaurants and shops, complaints should be addressed to the manager or proprietor. For more serious affairs, contact the police or your consulate.

CRIME AND SAFETY (See also EMERGENCIES and POLICE)

Austria's crime and theft rate is quite low compared to other parts of Europe. Nevertheless it is advisable not to leave valuable objects – especially cameras – in your car, which should always be left locked. If your passport is stolen, the police will give you a certificate to take to your consulate.

I want to report a theft.	**Ich möchte einen Diebstahl melden.**

CUSTOMS *(Zoll)* AND ENTRY REQUIREMENTS

A valid passport is required for entry. Visitors from European Union (EU) countries, the US, Canada, Australia and New Zealand do not require a visa. See <www.austria.org.uk> for further information from the Austrian Embassy in London.

The following items may be imported into Austria free of customs duties: 200 cigarettes or 50 cigars or 250g tobacco; 2 litres of alcohol (of less than 22 percent), and 1 litre of alcohol (of more than 22 percent). Citizens of EU member states are allowed to import larger quantities for their own use.

Currency restrictions. There are no restrictions on the import and export of national and foreign currencies.

VAT reimbursement. For purchases over a specified amount, non-EU citizens are entitled to reclaim the value-added tax *(Mehrwertsteuer)* if you are taking the goods out of the EU. The salesperson must complete form 'U 34', which you will need to present on departure to airport or border customs officials for stamping. Then you can post the form to the shop for reimbursement by cheque or bank-order.

I've nothing to declare.	**Ich habe nichts zu verzollen.**
It's for my personal use.	**Das ist für meinen persönlichen Gebrauch.**

D

DRIVING (See also CAR RENTAL/HIRE)

To bring your car into Austria you will need:

   valid driving licence (national licence for Europeans);
   car registration papers;
   national identity sticker for your car;
   red warning triangle in case of breakdown;
   first-aid kit.

Road conditions are by and large very good in Austria, only remote country roads are not paved.

Driving regulations. Drive on the right, pass on the left. Although drivers in Austria follow the same basic rules which apply in other countries that drive on the right, there are some rules that might differ somewhat:

• you must wear seat-belts;

• children under the age of 12 may not sit in front, and must use a special safety seat;

• on the motorway *(Autobahn)* passing another vehicle on its right is prohibited;

• vehicles coming from the right have priority at crossroads without other signals;

• trams have priority, even when coming from the left;

• vehicles must halt behind trams when they are slowing down to stop and when loading or unloading passengers;

• it is prohibited to use your horn (day or night) in town;

• motorcyclists must wear crash helmets and use dipped headlights throughout the day;

• drunken driving is a very serious offence in Austria. The permissible alcohol level in the blood is 0.8 percent.

Speed limits. On motorways (expressways) 130km/h (81mph) or 100km/h (62mph); on other roads 100km/h or 80km/h (50mph); in built-up areas 50km/h (31mph); with caravan (trailer) 80km/h (50mph) on the open road; with studded tires 100km/h (62mph) on motorways, 80km/h (50mph) on other roads.

Parking. In streets with tram tracks, parking is prohibited from 8pm to 5am from mid-December to the end of March to allow for

driving licence	**Führerschein**
car registration papers	**Zulassungsschein**
green card	**Grüne Karte**
Where's the nearest car park, please?	**Wo ist der nächste Parkplatz, bitte?**
Can I park here?	**Darf ich hier parken?**
Are we on the right road for...?	**Sind wir auf der richtigen Strasse nach...?**
Check the oil/tires/battery, please.	**Öl/Reifen/Batterie prüfen, bitte.**
I've had a breakdown.	**Ich habe eine Panne.**
There's been an accident.	**Es ist ein Unfall passiert.**

snow clearance. If at all possible, use public transport within the Gürtel (outer ring road) since one-way streets and traffic jams add confusion within the city, where there is a real lack of parking space. To park in 'blue' zones you will need parking tickets, valid from 8am to 6pm for up to 90 minutes. Tickets are available in banks and tobacco shops *(Tabaktrafik)*.

Breakdowns. Austrian automobile clubs offer 24-hour breakdown service to all drivers on motorways and main roads; ÖAMTC, tel: 120 <www.oeamtc.at>; ARBÖ, tel: 123 <www.arboe.at>.

Fuel and oil. There are plenty of petrol stations, some of them self-service. In Vienna, most service stations close at night, but you can fill up very late at the main entrances to the city.

Road signs. Most road signs employed in Austria are international, but here are some written signs you might come across:

Anfang	(Parking) Start	**Licht einschalten**	Use headlights
Ausfahrt	Exit		
Aussicht	Viewpoint	**Ortsende**	Town ends
Bau-arbeiten	Road works	**Parken erlaubt**	Parking allowed
Einbahn-strasse	One way	**Rechts, links einbiegen**	Turn right, left
Ende	(Parking) End	**Rollsplitt**	Loose gravel
Fahrbahn-wechsel	Change lanes	**Sackgasse**	No through road
Fussgänger	Pedestrians	**Spital**	Hospital
Gefahr	Danger (detour)	**Steinschlag**	Falling stones
Geradeaus	Straight on	**Umleitung**	Diversion
Glatteis	Slippery roads	**Vorfahrt**	Priority
Halten-Verboten	No stopping	**Vorsicht**	Caution
		Werktags von 7 bis 17 Uhr	Weekdays 7am to 5pm
		Zufahrt gestattet	Entrance permitted

E

ELECTRICITY

You'll need an adapter for most British and US plugs: Austrian sockets have round holes. Electricity supplies are 220 volt, and US equipment will require a transformer. Shaver outlets are generally dual voltage.

EMBASSIES AND CONSULATES

Contact your consulate or embassy only for real emergencies, such as loss of a passport or all your money, a serious accident or trouble with the police.

Australia Mattiellistrasse 2, A-1040 Vienna, tel: 50674.
Canada Laurenzerberg 2, 1010 Vienna, tel: 531 383000,
Ireland Rotenturmstrasse 16–18, 1010 Vienna, tel: 715 4246.
New Zealand Springsiedelgasse 28, 1090 Vienna, tel: 318 8505.
UK Jauresgasse 12, 1030 Vienna, tel: 71613-0.
US (Embassy) Boltzmanngasse 16, 1090 Vienna, tel: 31339-0; (Consulate) Gartenbaupromenade 2, 1010 Vienna, tel: 512 5835.

EMERGENCIES (See also CRIME AND SAFETY and POLICE)

If your hotel receptionist isn't at hand, the Viennese telephone service has several emergency numbers. The most important ones are listed below. If you do not speak German, try in English or find someone who speaks German to help you to call. See also HEALTH AND MEDICAL CARE.

Police emergency **133**
Fire **122**
Ambulance, first aid **144**
Pharmacist on duty **1550**
Emergency medical service **141**
Emergency dentist **512 2078**

I need a doctor/dentist.	**Ich brauche einen Arzt/ Zahnarzt.**
ambulance	**Krankenwagen**
Fire!	**Feuer!**
Help!	**Hilfe!**
hospital	**Spital**
police	**Polizei**

G

GAY AND LESBIAN TRAVELLERS

This sophisticated capital has a relatively friendly attitude towards gays and lesbians. Since 1996, the Regenbogen (Gay Rainbow) Parade has been held every June on the Ringstrasse. A list of restaurants, hotels and bars which welcome gays and lesbians is provided in the *Gay City Map,* available at some bars and hotels or directly from the publisher: BG Verlag, Mariahilferstrasse 123/3, 1060 Vienna. Two meeting places: Hosi Zentrum, Novaragasse 40. 1040 Wien, tel: 216 6604, <www.hosiwien.at>, and Rosa Lila Villa, 6, Linke Wienzeile 102, tel: 586 8150, <www.villa.at>.

GETTING THERE

Although the information below has been carefully checked, it is always advisable to consult a travel agent to verify exact times, fares and other arrangements.

By Air
Scheduled flights. There is regular service to Vienna from various centres in the UK. Austrian Airlines <www.aua.com> operates scheduled flights from Heathrow; British Airways <www.ba.com> has flights from Heathrow and Gatwick and Lauda-Air <www.laudaair.com> from Gatwick. Flying time from London is two and a half hours. The low-cost airline Ryanair <www.ryanair.com>

operates a service to Salzburg. The train journey from Salzburg to Vienna takes three hours. Various firms offer Vienna as a city break.

In addition to non-stop flights from New York and Chicago, there is a scheduled service from more than 40 American cities as well as a dozen cities in Canada to European gateway destinations from which you can make connections to Vienna.

Charter flights. Cheap charter flights are available from the UK. Accommodation is not generally included.

Charters operate from a selection of North American cities, including ABC (Advanced Booking Charter) flights and OTC (One-Stop Inclusive Tour Charter) package deals, which include return flights, hotel accommodation, selected meals and sightseeing. In addition, a number of British and American tour operators have individual and group packages to Austria offering stays of from two days to two weeks in Vienna. Consult your travel agent for details.

By Car

The quickest route to Vienna from the UK is via Calais through Brussels, Cologne, Nuremburg, Passau and Linz, although there are more attractive routes, such as *die romantische Strasse* (the Romantic Road), via Rothenburg ob der Tauber, through the countryside. There are regular daily car ferry departures from Dover to Calais, or you can put your car on the train and travel through the Channel Tunnel from Folkestone to Calais in 35 minutes.

Depending from which direction you come, you might be able to put your car on the train for part of the journey. In the summer a car-train *(Autozug)* service links Vienna with cities in Germany and Italy. Arriving with the car-train allows you to avoid traffic jams around Vienna and brings you close to the town centre.

The Austrian Federal Railways <www.oebb.at> operates car-trains between Vienna and Bischofshofen, Feldkirch (overnight service with couchettes also available), Linz, Villach and Innsbruck and Salzburg (both during the skiing season only).

By Rail

The Ostend–Vienna express takes about 16 hours; the entire trip, London to Vienna, takes about 24 hours. Couchettes and sleepers are available, but must be reserved in advance. Contact Rail Europe for details <www.raileurope.co.uk>.

The Austrian National Railpass *(Bundes-Netzkarte)* allows unlimited travel on Austrian Railways for one month. Contact Austrian Federal Railways for details <www.oebb.at>.

By Coach

For details of coach services to Vienna from London and other European cities contact Eurolines <www.eurolines.co.uk>.

GUIDES AND TOURS *(Fremdenführer; Rundfahrten)*

The most romantic tour of Vienna is in the famous horse-drawn *Fiaker* cab. These are usually parked at the Heldenplatz, Stephansplatz, or near the Albertina and will take you around the major sightseeing spots – the younger drivers may provide a running commentary in English as you ride. Make sure you agree on the cost of the trip before you begin. The price of a tram ticket will take you right round the Ringstrasse, but without commentary.

Vienna-Line bus tours, with an English-speaking hostess, are conveniently run on a hop-on/hop-off basis at 13 stops along the sightseeing route, starting from the Staatsoper. An uninterrupted tour lasts 2½ hours, but you can spread it over two days. Tickets can be purchased in many hotels or from Vienna Sightseeing Tours, *3, Stelzhammergasse 4/11, tel: 712 46 83 0.*

The Tourist Information Board organises guided **theme tours on foot** *(Wiener Spaziergänge* <www.wienguide.at>), often with English-speaking guides. Each tour lasts approximately 90 minutes. They cover all manner of special interests: Medieval Vienna, Hundertwasser and modern architecture, Jewish Vienna, *Jugendstil*, Amusing Vienna with tales and anecdotes. One particularly interesting walk is the *Musikmeile* (Music Mile). This is a classical music walk from Theater an der Wien to Stephansplatz, following stars embedded in the pavement that commemorate great personalities of classical music. You can also enjoy *Verliebt in Wien* (Vienna with love) and *Der Dritte Mann* (The Third Man), which follows in the footsteps of the film (which is shown quite often at the Burgkino, <www. burgkino.at>). There are guided tours of the sewers as well, but if all this is too sobersided, why not try *Ein luderleben der liebesdienerinnen* (The Erotic Vienna: a dissolute life of the tart)? Or alternatively, the Josefine Mutsenbacher Walk, which is humorous and deemed unsuitable for children, despite the bestseller about Josefine's life having been written by Felix Salten, the author renowned for writing *Bambi*.

There are also tram and boat tours.

Most hotels can arrange for English-speaking guides or interpreters. Or contact:

Vienna Guide Service, Sommerhaidenweg 124, tel: 440 3094, fax: 440 2825, <www.vienna-guide-service.com>.

We'd like an English-speaking guide.	**Wir möchten einen englischsprachigen Fremdenführer.**
I need an English interpreter.	**Ich brauche einen Dolmetscher für Englisch.**
How long will the ride take?	**Wie lange dauert die Fahrt?**
What does it cost?	**Was kostet es?**

H

HEALTH AND MEDICAL CARE *(Ärztliche Hilfe)*

You should have few worries in Vienna. Its doctors are among the best in Europe and the tap water is perfectly safe to drink. Ask your insurance company before leaving home if medical treatment in

Austria is covered by your policy. Pack whatever prescription drugs you may need, as you may not find exactly the same in Vienna. If you are a resident of an EU country you should obtain form E111 from your local post office before travelling or you will be liable to pay the full cost of medical treatment.

Most pharmacies *(Apotheke)* are open Monday to Friday and Saturday morning *(see* OPENING HOURS). For night and Sunday service, pharmacies display the address of the nearest shop remaining on duty. To find out which are open, tel: **1550**. (See also EMERGENCIES)

Where is there a pharmacy on duty?	**Wo ist die diensthabende Apotheke?**

L

LANGUAGE

Austria is German-speaking, but English is also very widely understood and spoken. If you don't speak German, don't forget to ask *'Sprechen Sie Englisch?'* (Do you speak English?) before plunging ahead. A gentle effort at *'Entschuldigen Sie bitte'* (Excuse me, please) gets you a long way. The *Berlitz German Phrase Book and Dictionary* covers most situations you're likely to encounter in Austria.

LAUNDRY AND DRY-CLEANING

Getting your clothes washed or cleaned by the hotel is costly. It's worth seeking out local dry-cleaners or self-service laundries. The *Gelbe Seiten* (Yellow Pages) list addresses under *Wäschereien* (laundries) and *Putzereien* (dry-cleaners), or ask your hotel reception.

When will it be ready?	**Wann ist es fertig?**
For tomorrow morning, please.	**Bis morgen früh, bitte.**

LOST PROPERTY *(Fundamt)*

The city lost property office is at Wasagasse 22, tel: 313 44 92 11; open Mon–Fri, 8am–noon.

I've lost my passport/ wallet/handbag	**Ich habe meinen Pass/meine Brieftasche/Handtasche verloren.**

M

MAPS

The Tourist Information Board gives away excellent street-maps of the city. Most useful will always be a large-scale map of the *Innere Stadt* (Inner City) and of the U-Bahn network. The one other place for which you will need a map is the Kunsthistorisches (Fine Arts) Museum – they can be obtained for free at the information desk.

MEDIA

Major hotels and most kiosks in the First District sell English-language daily newspapers from London, *International Herald Tribune*, *Wall Street Journal* and *USA Today*, and the news magazines.

TV in the major hotels usually has CNN and BBC World news services, along with other major European channels. Shortwave radio enthusiasts can get BBC World Service and VOA – check appropriate wavelengths before leaving home.

Vienna Tourist Board's *Monatsprogramm* provides full monthly cultural listings. German-speakers get a less formal, fresher view of the city's events, along with a full restaurant guide, with the first-rate monthly *Falter* magazine (similar to London's *Time Out* or New York's *Village Voice*).

MONEY MATTERS *(Geld)*

Austria's monetary unit is the euro, symbolised €. The euro is divided into 100 cents. Banknotes in denominations of 5, 10, 20, 50, 100, 200 and 500 euros are in circulation. There are coins to the value of 1 and 2 euros and 1, 2, 5, 10, 20 and 50 cents.

Banks and currency exchange. Foreign currency can be changed in practically all banks and savings banks *(Sparkasse)*. You can also change money at travel agencies and hotels, but the rate will not be as good. The quickest way to obtain cash is to use one of the many ATMs *(Automat)*. Major credit cards are accepted in most hotels, restaurants and shops in the tourist districts.

Bureaux de change are usually open from early morning (some from 6.30am) until late afternoon or evening. Some are open at the weekend, including those at the airport, Südbahnhof, Westbahnhof, City Air Terminal, Stephansplatz and Opernpassage.

Travellers' cheques *(Reisescheck)* are welcome almost every-where, but, again, the rates are best in banks.

I want to change some pounds/dollars	**Ich möchte Pfund/ Dollar wechseln.**
Do you accept travellers' cheques?	**Nehmen Sie Reisescheks an?**
Do you have any change, please?	**Haben Sie Kleingeld, bitte?**
Where's the nearest ATM, please?	**Wo ist der nächste Geldautomat, bitte**

O

OPENING HOURS

Shops. Most small places are open from 9am (grocery stores an hour earlier) to 6pm with a break for lunch. Major department stores do business from 8am–6pm, and in some cases 8pm, but supermarkets close for about two hours at lunch. Most shops close on Saturday afternoon, though some remain open until 5pm. Most shops remain closed on Sunday. Shops in railway stations are open daily 7am–10.30pm.

Museums. Hours vary considerably (see individual listings in the Where to Go section).

Banks. Mon–Fri 8am–3pm (Thur to 5.30pm). Most branches close 12.30–1.30pm.

Post offices Mon–Fri 8am–6pm. For 24-hour service, see POST OFFICE.

Pharmacies Mon–Fri 8am–noon, 2–6pm; Sat 8am–noon.

P

POLICE *(Polizei)* (See also CRIME AND SAFETY and EMERGENCIES)

Vienna's police wear green caps and jackets with black trousers, and drive white cars. Traffic police wear white caps and, in summer, white jackets. Street parking is supervised by *Politessen* (traffic wardens) in blue jackets and white hats. Police on motorcycles are popularly known as 'white mice' *(weisse Mäuse)*. If you are fined for any reason, the police have the right to ask you to pay on the spot. In emergencies, call **133**.

Where is the nearest police station, please?	**Wo ist die nächste Polizeiwachstube, bitte?**

POST OFFICE *(Postamt)*

Apart from regular post office hours, post offices at main railway stations (Westbahnhof, Südbahnhof and Franz Josefs-Bahnhof) are open day and night. Other offices offering this 24-hour service for registered, air and express mail (with a small extra charge): Central

Post Office, Fleischmarkt 19, and Central Telegraph Office, Börse-platz 1. Stamps are also available at tobacco shops *(Tabaktrafik)*.

express (special delivery)	**Express/Eilbote**
airmail	**Luftpost**
Have you any mail for...?	**Haben Sie Post für...?**
A stamp for this letter/ postcard, please.	**Eine Marke für diesen Brief/ diese Postkarte, bitte.**
I want to fax a letter to...	**Ich möchte einen Brief nach... faxen.**

PUBLIC HOLIDAYS *(Feiertage)*

Austria observes 14 public holidays a year on which banks, muse-ums, official services and many restaurants are closed. On Good Friday, a holiday for Protestants only, shops remain open.

January 1	*Neujahrstag*	New Year's Day
January 6	*Heilige Drei Könige*	Twelfth Night
May 1	*Tag der Arbeit*	Labour Day
August 15	*Mariä Himmelfahrt*	Assumption
October 26	*Nationalfeiertag*	National Holiday
	(Tag der Fahne)	(Flag Day)
November 1	*Allerheiligen*	All Saints' Day
December 8	*Unbefleckte*	Immaculate
	Empfängnis	Conception
December 25	*Weihnachten*	Christmas Day
December 26	*Stefanstag*	St Stephen's Day
Movable dates:	*Karfreitag*	Good Friday
	Ostermontag	Easter Monday
	Christi Himmelfahrt	Ascension Day
	Pfingstmontag	Whit Monday
	Fronleichnam	Corpus Christi

On 24 December (Christmas Eve) theatres and cinemas are closed all day and shops, restaurants and coffee houses close at midday.

Are you open tomorrow?	**Haben Sie morgen geöffnet?**

PUBLIC TRANSPORT

Maps for buses, trams and U-Bahn (subway) are available at main stops as well as at the central public transport information offices at Karlsplatz and Stephansplatz.

Tickets can be bought from a conductor or a machine on trams and buses, from the booking office or a machine for mainline or city trains. A single ticket for a journey by tram, bus and underground, which covers changes made without interruption, costs €1.50. Discount tickets can be bought in advance from a tobacconist's (*Tabaktrafik*) or transport offices (*Verkehrsbetriebe*). Travel passes are available for 24 hours (€5) and 72 hours (€12).

Also worth considering is the Vienna Card, a 72-hour ticket currently costing €16.90, which is valid on all public transport and entitles the holder to discounts at museums and other attractions (see BUDGETING FOR YOUR TRIP).

Trams (*Strassenbahn*). With some 35 tram routes, this is Vienna's most important form of public transport. On most trams (and buses) the driver serves as the conductor. These vehicles carry a blue sign front and rear with the word *Schaffnerlos* (without conductor). If you have a ticket, enter by the door marked *Entwerter* and have it stamped; otherwise get in at the front and buy your ticket from the vending machine. For trams with conductors, enter at the rear to buy a ticket or have it stamped. The most useful lines are:

1 and 2 around the Ringstrasse.

38 from Schottentor to Grinzing.

52 and 58 from the Westbahnhof to the city centre.

Buses. The airport bus service runs between the City Air Terminal at Landstrasse Hauptstrasse (Hilton Hotel) and the airport every 20 or 30 minutes. Allow half-an-hour for the journey. The main city centre routes are:

1a from Schottentor to Stephansplatz.

2a from Burgring to Graben.

3a from Schottenring to Schwarzenbergplatz.

U-Bahn (underground). Five lines cover all the main parts of the city. Tickets can be purchased from machines or ticket offices. The lines are:

U1 Kagran–Stephansplatz–Karlsplatz–Reumannplatz.

U2 Schottenring–Volkstheater–Karlsplatz.

U3 Ottakring–Stephansplatz–Landstrasse–Simmering.

U4 Hütteldorf–Karlsplatz–Schwedenplatz–Heiligenstadt.

U6 Floridsdorf–Spittelau–Westbahnhof–Meidling–Philadelphia-brücke–Siebenherten.

Schnellbahn (S-Bahn). Rapid transit suburban trains depart from the Südbahnhof for outlying districts. The unit fare applies in the central zone, standard fares outside. Other points of departure are Wien Nord and Wien Mitte. The S-Bahn also connects to the airport, as does the City Airport Train (CAT; see AIRPORT).

R

RELIGION

Austria is predominantly Roman Catholic. Sunday Mass in some churches is accompanied by orchestral and choral works. Consult a newspaper under *Kirchenmusik* for exact times.

English-language Catholic Mass is held at 11am at Votivkirche, Rooseveltplatz 8, tel: 408 5050 14.

There is an Anglican/Episcopal Church at Jauresgasse 17–19, tel: 720 7973.

Jewish services take place at the Stadttempel, Seitenstettengasse 4, tel: 531 0415.

T

TAXIS

As in any big city, Vienna never has enough taxis at rush hour, so book in advance through your hotel receptionist or by calling one of the following numbers: tel: 31 300/40 100/60 160. If you want to go beyond the city limits, negotiate the fare in advance.

TELEPHONES

Austria's country code is **43**, Vienna's area code is **(0)1**, dropping the 0 for calls from abroad. For **international calls** from Vienna, dial **00** before the country code (**44** for UK, **1** for US), then the area code and number of your destination.

Use call centres or telephone booths with pre-paid cards. Phone cards *(Telefonwertkarte)* are available from post offices and tobacconists; costs vary so shop around for the best buy. Telephone booths all have multilingual instructions. Calls are cheaper 6pm–8am and on Saturday, Sunday and public holidays. Hotels often charge double the public phone rate to make a call.

Directory enquiries (local)   11811
Directory enquiries (long-distance)   11814

TICKETS *(Karten)*

Music. Tickets for performances can be obtained at private ticket agencies *(Theaterkartenbüro)* throughout the city, as well as at major hotels, but these will cost at least 22 percent more. Try Vienna Ticket Service, 1043 Vienna, Postfach 160. tel: 43 1 587 98 43, fax: 43 1 587 98 44, Its website <www.wien.gv.at/english/> has links to the individual booking services of numerous cultural institutions and events, including music.

Tickets for the Saturday and Sunday as well as evening concerts of the Wiener Philharmoniker orchestra are only available through subscription and the waiting lists are years long. Tickets for other concerts performed by the orchestra can be booked in advance: Wiener Philharmoniker, Bösendorferstrasse 12, 1010 Vienna <www.wiener philharmoniker.at>.

Spanish Riding School. Ticket applications should be sent at least six months in advance to: Spanische Reitschule, Michaelerplatz 1, 1010 Vienna <www.spanische-reitschule.com>. Tickets can be bought on the day for the morning training sessions.

Opera and Theatre. The best place for opera tickets is the National Theatre ticket office *(Österreichischer Bundestheaterverband, Bestellbüro)*. It sells tickets seven days ahead for opera (Staatsoper), operetta (Volksoper), Burgtheater and Akademietheater performances (closed in July and August). You can reserve tickets at least three weeks before the performance by writing to: Bundestheaterkassen, Goethegasse 1, 1010 Vienna. For information the number to call is 43 1 514 44 29 59 or 43 1 514 44 29 60. Ticket sales by credit card are available six days in advance, tel: 43 1 513 1513, or fax: 43 1 514 44 2969. Standing-room tickets are sold for evening performances, at the box office prior to the performance.

Vienna Boys' Choir *(Wiener Sängerknaben)*. Obtain tickets in advance at the Hofburg Kapelle on Friday 5–7pm for Sunday performances, or reserve at least two months in advance from: Hofmusikkapelle, Hofburg, Schweizerhof, 1010 Vienna; <www.wsk.at>. The choir can also be heard every Friday at the Konzerthaus in May, June, September and October. Tickets are available from major hotels, or Reisebüro Mondial, Faulmanngasse 4, 1040 Vienna.

TIME ZONES

Austria is on Central European Time (GMT+1). In summer, clocks move ahead one hour, and the time difference looks like this:

New York	London	**Vienna**	Jo'burg	Sydney	Auckland
6am	11am	**noon**	noon	8pm	10pm

TIPPING

Since a service charge is included in hotel and restaurant bills, tipping is not obligatory, but it is customary to add a tip of about 10 percent to the bill.

It is also appropriate to give something extra to porters, cloakroom attendants and hotel maids for their services. Taxi drivers and hairdressers also expect a 10 percent tip.

TOILETS *(Toiletten)*

Public facilities can be found near important streets or squares, often in the pedestrian underpasses. Normally toilets in cafés can be used without ordering anything, but it is always more courteous to have a coffee or a beer. If hand towels and soap are used in public facilities, there is often a set fee rather than just tip. Have some small change ready in case the door is coin operated.

Toilets may be labelled with male or female pictograms, WC, or *Damen* (Ladies) and *Herren* (Gentlemen).

TOURIST INFORMATION

The Austrian National Tourist Office/ANTO *(die Österreichische Fremdenverkehrswerbung)* has comprehensive information about what to see, when to go, and where to stay in and around Vienna <www.austria-tourism.co.uk>.

Australia: ANTO, 1st Floor, 36 Carrington Street, Sydney NSW 2000. tel: 9299 3621, fax: 9299 3808.

Canada: ANTO, 2 Bloor Street East, Suite 3330, Toronto, Ontario M4W 1A8, tel: (416) 967-3381, fax: (416) 967-4101.

Ireland: ANTO, Merrion Centre, Nutley Lane, Dublin 4. tel: 01 283 0488, fax: 01 283 0531.

UK: ANTO, 14 Cork Street, London W1X 1PF. tel: 020 7629 0461, fax: 020 7499 6038.

US: ANTO, PO Box 1142, New York, NY 10108-1142. tel: 212 944 6880, fax: 212 730 4568.

Vienna Tourist Board

The Tourist Information Office is located right behind the Vienna State Opera at Albertinaplatz 1/corner of Maysedergasse, tel: 24 555, fax: 24 555 666; open 9am–7pm daily. The office is able to book tickets, make hotel reservations, organise sightseeing trips and change money. You can also make room reservations and request free brochures over the phone. The Vienna Tourist Board's website <www.info.wien.at> offers a monthly preview and comprehensive database of events, online booking for hotels and pensions, and information for visitors with disabilities.

TRAVELLERS WITH DISABILITIES

Vienna has implemented a great many schemes to enable wheelchair access. Most hotels have wheelchair access and some have rooms adapted for disabled people, though it would be wise to question the manager before making a reservation, to ensure that the room is suitable. Older buses and trams are not accessible, though many U-Bahn stations are. The Vienna Tourist Board can provide up-to-date information. It has a list of sights and attractions with wheelchair access. You'll be pleased to know that the *Riesenrad* (Ferris wheel) is accessible. Local voluntary organisations may also offer help.

Fahrtendienst Haas, Karl Schäferstrasse 6, A-1210, tel: 27700 ; fax: 27700/30, <www.members.aon.at/haas-bus>, provides transport for wheelchair users.

W

WEBSITES

The Vienna Tourist Board has an excellent website at <www. info.wien.at> with pages in seven languages, including English, that give comprehensive information about forthcoming cultural, sporting and social events. The board also has an email address to which you can send English-language queries: <inquiries@info.wien.at>.

For hotel reservations, e-mail to wienhotels@info.wien.at.

The Austrian Tourist Board site is <www.austria-tourism.at>.

The City of Vienna's website, <www.wien.gv.at>, lists information on all aspects of life in the city and is available in English.

German language news and useful information for visitors is at <www.wienweb.at>.

An extensive listing of children's information is at <www.kidsweb.at/wienweb>.

For city museums go to <www.museum-Vienna.at>.

For information about the Vienna Festival *(Wiener Festwochen)*, visit <www.festwochen.or.at>.

For your day-to-day planning for restaurants, entertainments and sight-seeing, visit the website of *Falter* magazine, the monthly guide to what's going on and going down in Vienna, <www.falter.at> (this site is in German only).

WEIGHTS AND MEASURES

Austria uses the metric system.

Y

YOUTH HOSTELS *(Jugendhgerberge)*

There is a large, modern hostel near the Danube as you enter Vienna from the north, with two and four beds to a room. You can obtain information about the other 100 hostels in Austria there.

Austrian Youth Hostels Association, Helfersdorferstrasse 4, A–1010 Vienna, tel: 43 1 533 1833, fax: 43 1 533 1833 85, <www.oejhw.or.at>

Jugendgästehaus, Friedrich-Engelsplatz 24, A–1200 Vienna, tel: 43 1 332 82 940, fax: 43 1 330 8379.

A popular backpacker's place is Wombats, Grangasse A-1150. tel 897 2336, fax: 897 2577, <www.wombats.at>, near Mariahilferstrasse. It's bright and breezy, cheap and cheerful; free linen and a welcome drink.

Recommended Hotels

Vienna's hotels compare in quality to those of other major European capitals. However, shortage of accommodation, particularly during peak season – Christmas and New Year, and from Easter to the end of September – does mean that advance booking is advisable. Reservations may be made by telephone (country code 43 followed by area code 1), fax, letter, or the Internet, and are binding even if not confirmed in writing.

The hotels listed here are placed in four categories based on the approximate price in euros per night for a double room with private bath or shower unless otherwise stated. A service charge and taxes are included in the price. Breakfast is also usually included, generally a buffet of various cold meats and cheeses, cereals, bread, rolls, jam and coffee. Always confirm prices when booking. All the hotels listed take major credit cards; wheelchair access where specified. The district number precedes the street address.

€€€€	over 200 euros
€€€	130–200 euros
€€	80–130 euros
€	under 80 euros

Academia Hotels € *Head office: 8, Pfeilgasse 3a, tel: 401 76 55, fax: 401 76 20; <www.academia-hotels.co.at>.* Academia Hotels are university halls of residence that open from July to September as *'saison hotels'*. They are quite centrally located, comfortable, clean and decent.

Admiral €€ *7, Karl-Schweighofer-Gasse 7, tel: 52 41 0; fax: 521 41 16; <www.admiral.co.at>.* Off Mariahilferstrasse, but quiet and soundproofed, this hotel is convenient for the art and foodie centre of Spittelburg and not far from the MuseumsQuartier and city centre. Rooms have e-mail modems and some have kitchenettes for longer and family stays. Wheelchair access. 78 rooms

Albertina Hotels € *Head office: Fürichgasse 10, A 1010 Vienna tel: 512 74 93; fax: 512 19 68; <www.albertina-hotels.at>.* University halls of residence which are available for accommodation from from July to September. Fairly central, clean and agreeable places to stay.

Am Brillantengrund €€–€€€ *7, Bandgasse 4, tel: 523 36 62; fax: 526 13 30; <www.hotel-am-brilliantengrund.at>.* Your chance to stay in a national monument on a quiet street near Maria-hilferstrasse, bedecked with flowers and plants. Internet access; wheelchair access. 31 rooms.

Am Schubertring €€€ *1, Schubertring 11, tel: 717 02 0; fax: 713 99 66; <www.schubertring.at>.* A renovated 19th-century mansion with rooms in the belle époque or art nouveau style. The hotel is between Musikverein and Stadtpark. Wheelchair access. 39 rooms.

Amadeus €€€ *1, Wildpretmarkt 5, tel: 533 87 38; fax: 533 87 38 38; <www.hotel-amadeus.at>.* A pleasant modern hotel behind a *Jugendstil* exterior in a quiet side street just 200m from the Stephansdom. 30 rooms.

ANA Grand Hotel Wien €€€€ *1, Kärntner Ring 9, tel: 515 80 0; fax: 515 13 13; <www.anagrand.com>.* One of the city's old-world institutions resurrected in 1994 as a modern luxury hotel. It is also the home of Unkai, Vienna's most exclusive Japanese restaurant. Facilities for disabled travellers. 205 rooms.

Ananas €€€ *5, Rechte Wienzeile 93–5, tel: 546 20 0; fax: 545 42 42; <www.austria-trend.at>.* Situated near Naschmarkt and Karl-splatz, this hotel has a distinctive *Jugendstil* exterior and a very pleasant interior. The restaurant Zum Moser is named after the fa-mous actor Hans Moser, who was born here. Facilities for the busi-ness traveller. Wheelchair access. 534 rooms.

Arcotel Boltzmann €€€ *9, Boltzmanngasse 8, tel: 316 12 0; fax: 316 12 81 6; <www.arcotel.at>.* Pleasant modern hotel decorated in young bright colours. The Freud Museum and Strudelhofsteig are close by. Wheelchair access. 70 rooms.

Arenberg €€€ *1, Stubenring 2, tel: 512 52 91; fax: 513 93 56; <www.arenberg.at>.* An excellent Best Western hotel on the Ringstrasse, near Donaukanal. It offers comfort, good breakfasts and old-world charm. Wheelchair access. 22 rooms.

Austria €€ *1, Wolfengasse 3/Fleischmarkt 20, tel: 515 23; fax: 515 23 50 6; <www.hotelaustria-wien.at>.* Elegant hotel situated on a quiet street in the city centre, beside the old Roman camp. Wheelchair access. 46 rooms.

Bristol €€€€ *1, Kärntner Ring 1, tel: 515 16 0; fax: 515 16 55 0; <www.westin.com/bristol>.* Offering unbridled luxury, the Bristol rates among the great hotels of the world. It has a new high-tech business centre and all the trimmings. Situated opposite the Opera, it is home to the highly regarded Korso and Sirk restaurants. Facilities for disabled travellers. 140 rooms.

De France €€€€ *1, Schottenring 3, tel: 313 68 0; fax: 319 59 69; <www.hoteldefrance.at>.* An elegant, up-to-date Ringstrasse hotel, close to the city centre, the cathedral and the Hofburg. Business guests are catered for. Its fine restaurants include the Bel Etage, Bistro, Sushi Bar and Atrium Café. Wheelchair access. 212 rooms.

Drei Kronen €€ *4, Schleifmühlgasse 25, tel: 587 32 89; fax: 587 32 89 11; <www.hotel3kronen.at>.* A family-run, art nouveau-style hotel named after the Austrian, Hungarian and Bohemian crowns on the side of the building. The hotel has been well refurbished. Conveniently situated near the Naschmarkt. 41 rooms.

Esterhazy € *6, Nelkengasse 3, tel: 587 51 59; fax: 585 79 88; <http://members.chello.at/pensionesterhazy>.* Modest pension in a quiet but central location just outside the Ringstrasse near the museums. Shared showers and toilets.

Ferchergasse Appartements € *7, Ferchergasse 19, tel: 484 45 22; fax: 484 45 22 20; <www.rohacek.at>.* The rooms are nicely furnished with fully-equipped kitchens. A good location for reaching the city and Wienerwald. Three nights minimum. 7 rooms.

Gartenhotel Glanzing €€–€€€ *19, Glanzinggasse 23, tel: 470 42 72 0; fax: 470 42 72 14; <www.gartenhotel-glanzing.at>.* Located in one of Vienna's smartest residential districts, this family-run hotel offers a room with a view and also a sauna, solarium, fitness room and garden. Child-friendly; wheelchair access. 17 rooms.

Haus Pillmeyer € *14, Sofienalpenstrasse 9, tel: 979 21 83; fax: 979 21 83; <www.pension-pillmeier.at>.* This is a chalet-style bed-and-breakfast in the Wienerwald, but with access to the city. Walking, riding and tennis nearby. 8 rooms.

Haus Sanz € *23, Krobothgasse 6, tel: 677 34 05; fax: 667 34 05 13; <www.haussanz>.* Family-run pension with pretty rooms and attentive service. Child friendly. 2 rooms.

Hilton Vienna Plaza €€€€ *1, Schottenring 11, tel: 313 90 2; fax: 313 90 22 00 9; <www.hilton.com>.* Centrally located on the Ring, close to the business, cultural and shopping districts. Suites are in various styles, including Hoffman, Frank Lloyd Wright and Mies van der Rohe. De luxe facilities; wheelchair access. 218 rooms.

Hilton Vienna Danube *(prices on request) 2, Handelskai 269, tel: 727 77 0; fax: 727 77 19 9; <www.vienna-danube.hilton.com>.* Situated beside the Danube in a former granary, this hotel is convenient for the exhibition grounds and the Prater. Shuttle-bus to the city centre; accommodation for disabled travellers. 367 rooms.

Ibis Wien Mariahilf €–€€ *6, Mariahilfer Gürtel 22-24, tel: 599 98; fax: 597 90 90; <www.ibishotel.com>.* Clean, comfortable, French chain hotel. Wheelchair access. 341 rooms.

Im Palais Schwarzenberg €€€€ *3, Schwarzenbergplatz 9, tel: 798 45 15; fax: 798 47 14; <www.palais-schwarzenberg.com>.* The last family-owned palace in Vienna, this imposing baroque building was designed by Lukas von Hildebrandt and Bernhard Fischer von Erlach. It's one of Vienna's most exclusive hotels, with its own park for tennis, jogging, walking and relaxing. The Terrassen is one of Vienna's finest restaurants. Wheelchair access. 44 rooms.

Imperial €€€€ *1, Kärntnerring 16, tel: 501 10 0; fax: 501 10 41 0; <www.luxurycollection.com/imperial>.* Opened in 1873 by Emperor Franz Joseph, this is the city's favourite celebrity hotel. Business services are as fine as you would anticipate. The *Imperial Torte* is a rival to Sacher's. Suitable for disabled travellers. 138 rooms.

Inter-Continental Wien €€€€ *3, Johannesgasse 28, tel: 711 22 0; fax: 713 44 89; <www.vienna.interconti.com>.* This luxury hotel near Stadtpark offers ultra-modern services. It has two new restaurants: Nobile prepares pasta and starters in an open kitchen and MediterraNeo offers elegant Mediterranean food. 453 rooms.

Jäger €€ *17, Hernalser Hauptstrasse 187, tel: 486 66 20 0; fax: 486 66 20 8; <www.bestwestern-ce.com/jaeger>.* Located in western Vienna, the hotel has been run by the Jäger family for 80 years. It's family-friendly (offering spacious apartments) and caters for the business traveller. Direct tram link into the city centre. 18 rooms.

Kaffeemühle Pension € *7, Kaiserstrasse 45, tel: 523 86 88; 526 48 61; fax: 523 86 88 17; <www.kaffeemuehle.at>.* A cheerful family-run *pension* located off Mariahilferstrasse. 16 rooms.

Kaiserin Elisabeth €€ *1, Weihburggasse 3, tel: 515 26; fax: 515 26 7; <wwwkaiserinelisabeth.at>.* Historic building beloved by composers Liszt and Wagner. Biedermeier furniture. 63 rooms.

Kaiserpark Schönbrunn €€–€€€ *12, Grünbergstrasse 11, tel: 813 86 10 0; fax: 813 81 83; <www.kaiserpark.at>.* A pleasant family-run hotel in a former guest house for Schönbrunn, built in 1903. Good transport links. Wheelchair access. 45 rooms.

Kärntnerhof €€–€€€ *1, Grashofgasse 4, tel: 512 19 23; fax: 513 22 28 33; <www.karntnerhof.com>.* Attractive old building situated in a lively area of the First District, but in a quiet cul-de-sac. Wheelchair access. 43 rooms.

Karolinenhof €€ *21, Jedleseer Strasse 75, tel: 278 78 01; fax: 278 78 01 8; <www.karolinenhof.at>.* Rare family-owned hotel located in Florisdorf, trans-Danube Vienna. Ideal for families wanting to enjoy Donauinsel's swimming and sport, but also suitable for business guests. Wheelchair access. 44 rooms.

Klimt €€ *14, Felbigergasse 58, tel: 914 55 65; 911 19 42; fax :911 19 42 5; <www.klimt-hotel.at>.* Renovated in the *Jugendstil* style, this hotel offers the unusual option for guests to order special mattresses on request. Fabulous honeymoon suite with canopied bed. Snack bar with meals available. Wheelchair access. 24 rooms.

König von Ungarn €€€ *1, Schulerstrasse 10, tel: 515 84 0; fax: 515 84 8; <www.kvu.at>.* Charming 16th-century mansion on a quiet street near Stephansdom in the Figarohaus complex. Take breakfast in the pretty winter garden. Wheelchair access. 33 rooms.

Kraml € *6, Brauergasse 5, tel: 587 85 88; fax: 586 75 73; <www. pensionkraml.at>.* A family-run pension close to Mariahilferstrasse and 15-minutes' walk from the Westbahnhof and the Ring. Clean and friendly, with a small courtyard and trees. 14 rooms.

Landhaus Furhgassl-Huber €€ *19, Rathstrasse 24, tel: 440 30 33; fax: 440 27 14; <www.fuhrgassl-huber.at>.* This hotel is at Neustift am Walde, an area of vineyards and *heuriger* within the city limits. Once the town hall, the interior is by Walter von Hoessl, stage designer for the State Opera. Wheelchair access. 38 rooms.

Le Meridien Vienna €€€€ *1, Opernring 13-15, tel: 588 90 0; fax: 588 90 90 90; <www.lemeridien.com>.* Cutting edge designer hotel behind a listed façade close to the Opera House. Top-class gastronomic pleasures in the restaurant. 261 rooms, 33 suites.

Mailbergerhof €€€–€€€€ *1, Annagasse 7, tel: 512 06 41; fax: 512 06 41 10; <www.mailbergerhof.at>.* Historic building in the city centre, once owned by the Knights Hospitallers. A nicely furnished, family-run hotel with a delightful inner courtyard. 40 rooms.

Marriott Vienna €€€–€€€€ *1, Parkring 12a, tel: 515 18 0; fax: 515 18 67 36; <www.marriott.com>.* The hotel is built in dramatic postmodern style on the Ringstrasse, opposite Stadtpark. It caters for the business traveller. Suitable for disabled travellers. 313 rooms.

Mozart Pension €–€€ 6, *Theobaldgasse 15, tel: 587 85 05; fax: 587 85 05; <www.pension-mozart.at>.* A traditional Viennese-furnished *pension* near the Naschmarkt. Helpful staff. 14 rooms.

Museum €€ 1, *Museumstrasse 3, tel: 523 44 26 0; fax: 523 44 26 30; <www.tiscover.com/hotel.museum>.* A pretty, late 19th-century building opposite the Natural History and Fine Arts museums. Some of the rooms have a balcony. 15 rooms.

Novotel Wien West €€ 14, *Am Auhof, tel: 979 25 42 0; fax: 979 41 40; <www.novotel.com>.* Comfortable, friendly hotel which welcomes families and business people. Wheelchair access. 112 rooms.

Parkhotel Schönbrunn €€€ 13, *Hietzinger Hauptstrasse 10–20, tel: 878 04 0; fax: 878 04 32 20; <www.austria-trend.at>.* Franz Joseph's former guest house, the building blends imperial atmosphere with modern facilities. Grand balls take place in the glittering ballroom. Irresistible! Wheelchair access. 402 rooms.

Pertschy Pension €€–€€€ 1, *Habsburgergasse 5, tel: 534 49 0; fax: 534 49 49; <www.pertschy.com>.* This *pension*, situated in the one-time Palais Cavriani (1734), is much sought after. 50 rooms.

Quisisana € 6 *Windmühlgasse 6, tel: 587 33 41; fax: 587 71 56 33; <www.quisisana-wien.co.at>.* A family-run hotel in *Jugdenstil* style, just a block from Mariahilferstrasse. 16 rooms.

Residenz Pension €–€€ 1, *Ebendorferstrasse 10, tel: 406 47 86 0; fax: 406 47 86 50; <www.residenz.cc>.* An excellent position between the Town Hall and the Ringstrasse university buildings. Free internet access in rooms. Wheelchair access. 15 rooms.

Sacher Wien €€€€ 1, *Philharmonikerstrasse 4, tel: 514 56; fax: 514 56 81 0; <www.sacher.com>.* A *fin de siècle* gem, founded in 1876. It offers unashamed luxury. Wheelchair access. 113 rooms.

Schloss Wilhelminenberg €€€ *Austria Trend Hotel, Savoyen-strasse 2, tel: 485 85 03; fax: 485 48 76; <www.austria-trend.at>.* This recently-refurbished, former hunting lodge in the Vienna Woods has a large garden. Wheelchair access. 87 rooms.

Sophienalpe € *14, Sofienalpenstrasse 13, tel: 486 24 32, fax: 485 16 55 12; <www.sophienalpe.at>.* A country hotel, a 20-km (12-mile) drive from the city centre, originally built by Franz Joseph as a summer house for his mother, Duchess Sophie. It offers good food, comfy rooms and a pool, and is an absolute bargain. Wheelchair access. 70 rooms.

Suzanne €€ *1, Walfischgasse 4, tel: 513 25 07; fax: 513 25 00; <www.pension-suzanne.at>.* Two generations of the Strafinger family have been working to provide a pleasant stay in their spacious apartments with *fin-de-siècle* style furnishings. The pension is close to the Opera and city centre. Wheelchair access. 25 rooms.

Urania €€ *3, Obere Weissbergergasse 7, tel: 713 17 11; fax: 713 56 94; <www.hotel-urania.at>.* The rooms are in different styles: choose from Jugendstil, Baroque, medieval and oriental among others. Close by are the Hundertwasser House, Prater and the Austria Centre (exhibition/conference centre). Wheelchair access. 32 rooms.

Wandl €€–€€€ *1, Petersplatz 9, tel: 534 55 0; fax: 534 55 77; <www.hotel-wandl.com>.* Situated just off Graben, this hotel was built in 1700 as the home of a Court Chamber official. It's now a family-run establishment, conscious of tradition and with an elegant staircase for you to sweep down. Wheelchair access. 138 rooms.

Zipser €€ *8, Lange Gasse 49, tel: 404 54 0, fax: 404 54 13; <www.zipser.at>.* This is a good, comfortable tourist hotel, conveniently located for the university, museums and Hofburg. Internet access; wheelchair access. 47 rooms.

Zur Wiener Staatsoper €€ *1, Krugerstrasse 11, tel: 513 12 74, fax: 513 12 74 15; <www.zurwienerstaatsoper.at>.* A family-run hotel in a gracious, flower-covered building by the Opera. 22 rooms.

Recommended Restaurants

Dining out has always been a popular pastime in Vienna. It is part of Austrian culture to take the family out for lunch at the weekend and to meet friends in a *Beisl* (convivial Viennese equivalent of the bistro) or at the *Heuriger* wine garden. In restaurants, the emphasis is on good company, good wine, robust portions and, usually, reasonable prices – a dramatically different approach from many other European capitals.

When choosing a restaurant, something to bear in mind during the summer months is whether you can sit outside in a garden or *Schanigarten* (tables on the pavement with sunshades). If you're simply after a quick snack, then look for a *Würstelstand*, a small kiosk selling sausages and other local specialities, such as *Leberkäsesemmel* (liver pâté sandwich). These kiosks are to be found on street corners all over the city *(see page 92)*.

Restaurants are listed alphabetically. Price categories are based on the cost, per person, of a dinner comprising starter, mid-priced main course and dessert (not including wine, coffee, or service) and are indicated as follows:

€€€   40–75 euros

€€   15–40 euros

€   15 euros and under

Heuriger, Stadtheuriger and cafés are listed on pages 138–142. Cafés serve meals in the € category unless otherwise specified.

Achilleus € *1, Köllnerhofgasse 3, tel. 512 83 28.* Tucked away in a small side street in the 'Bermuda Triangle' area of Vienna, this is one of the city's best Greek restaurants, prices reasonable, service exceptionally friendly. Open Mon–Fri dinner only, 5.30pm–midnight; Sat/Sun also lunch 11.30am–3pm, dinner 5.30pm–midnight.

Bodega Marques €€ *1, Parisergasse 1, tel: 533 91 70;* <www.marques.at>. The Bodega is housed in one of Vienna's oldest palaces, Palais Collalto. It serves Spanish *tapas*, Serrano ham, grilled lamb chops and Mediterranean-style food accompanied by good Spanish wine. Mon–Sat 5pm–1am.

Brasserie Ruben's €€ *1, Furstengasse 1, tel: 319 23 96*. The restaurant and brasserie attractively set in the grounds of the Liechtenstein Museum offers traditional Austrian food such as beef, dumplings, trout and veal. Wed–Sun 11am–midnight.

Café Sacher Wien €€€ *1, Philharmonikerstrasse 4, tel: 514 56 0; <www.sacher.com>*. One of Vienna's top restaurants, a classic and the place from whence the *torte* set forth to conquer the world. Daily lunch; dinner 6pm–11.30pm.

Do & Co €€€ *1, Stephansplatz 12; tel: 535 39 69; <www.doco.com>*. Refined Viennese and international cuisine in the Haas-Haus opposite the cathedral,Daily lunch; dinner 6pm–midnight. A branch has opened at *Albertinaplatz 1, tel: 532 96 69*.

Figlmüller €€ *1, Wollzeile 5, tel: 512 61 77; <www.figlmuller.com>*. This long-established institution, founded 1905, has branches at Bäckerstrasse and Grinzinger Strasse. It serves the ultimate *Wienerschnitzel*, so big that it overlaps the plate. The wines are from its own vineyard. Daily 11am–11.30pm (closed July).

G–town: The Gasometers €–€€ *<www.g-town.at>*. Twenty restaurants await you, catering for all tastes and purses.

Gösser Bierklinik € *1, Steindlgasse 4, tel: 535 68 97*. A comfortable place in a beautiful medieval building. You can view a cannonball which the Turks hurled during the siege of Vienna. However, you might also be lured by fine wines and substantial meals, *schnitzel* and sausages featured here. Mon–Sat 10am–11.30pm.

Griechenbeisl €€ *1, Fleischmarkt 11, tel: 533 19 77, <www.griechenbeisl.at>*. 'Greek' only in name, because that was its clientele 200 years ago. Today it serves traditional fare in one of Vienna's oldest houses (1447). *Schanigarten*. Daily 11am–1am.

GulaschMuseum €€ *1, Schulerstrasse 20, tel: 512 10 17; fax: 512 10 18; <www.gulasch.at>.* And now for something completely different: this 'museum' offers more than 15 types of *gulasch*, from tripe to chocolate. Mon–Fri 9am–midnight, Sat–Sun 10am–midnight.

Hansen €€ *1, Wipplingerstrasse 34, tel: 532 05 42; fax 532 05 42 10; <www.hansen.co.at>.* Enjoy breakfast, a light lunch or dinner in the Mediterranean atmosphere of this restaurant in the basement beneath the Stock Exchange. Mon–Fri 9am–9pm (hot meals till 8pm), Sat 9am–5pm (hot meals till 3pm).

Korso bei der Oper €€€ *1, Mahlerstrasse 5, tel: 515 16 54 6; <www.westin.com/bristol>.* A beautiful restaurant for discerning diners in the sumptuous surroundings of the Hotel Bristol. The food is light, innovative, seasonal and on a Viennese theme. Piano music accompaniment. Sun–Fri noon–2pm, 6pm–11pm, Sat 6pm–11pm.

K.u.K. Restaurant Piaristenkeller € *Kaiser Franz Joseph Hut–Museum, 8, Piaristengasse 45, tel: 406 01 93; <www.piaristen keller.co.at>.* Viennese cuisine using recipes from the emperor's days. The setting is a candle–lit monastery cellar and there's zither music, concerts, dancing and entertainment. Mon–Sat 6pm–11pm.

Ma'estro €€ *3, Am Heumarkt 6, tel: 714 89 11; fax: 242 00 72 1; <www.restaurant-maestro.at>.* This restaurant in the Konzerthaus is in the hands of a talented young chef. It offers exceptional cuisine in a pleasant atmosphere. Mon–Sat, 5.30pm–midnight.

Oswald und Kalb €€ *1, Bäckerstrasse 14, tel: 512 13 71.* Fashionable upmarket *Beisl* serving Styrian wine and cuisine. It is known for its beef in vinegar and pumpkin-seed oil. Daily 6pm–2am.

Terrassenrestaurant Palais Schwarzenberg €€€ *3, Hotel im Palais Schwarzenberg; Schwarzenbergplatz 9; tel: 798 45 15 0; <www.palais-schwarzenberg.com>.* Housed in a baroque palace, this restaurant is truly special, with a classic interior and views over an exquisite garden. The food is beautifully prepared and presented. Daily, lunch noon–2.30pm, dinner 6pm–10.30pm.

Palatschinkenkuchl € *1, Köllnerhofgasse 4; tel: 512 31 05*. An unpretentious place, which is popular with children as it serves a variety of sweet and savoury pancakes and milkshakes. Mon–Sat 10am–midnight, Sun 5pm–midnight.

Palmenhaus im Burggarten € *1, Burggarten 1 (entrance to Albertina), tel: 533 10 33; fax: 533 10 33 10; <www.palmenhaus.at>*. A chic place to eat, in an imperial glasshouse between the Albertina and the Butterfly House. 10am–1am (hot meals till midnight).

Palais-Restaurant Daun-Kinsky €€€ *1, Freyung 4, tel: 532 71 21; fax 532 62 71 50; <www.haslauer.at>*. Mediterranean food with an Asian touch, served in a baroque palace. Lavish is the word. Mon–Sat noon–1am (hot meals noon–2.30pm and 6.30–10–30pm).

Plachutta €€ *1, Wollzeile 38, tel: 512 15 77; <www. plachutta. at>*. Haute cuisine versions of Viennese specialities include a *Tafelspitz* fit for an emperor. Daily 11.30am–11.15pm.

Salzamt €€ *1, Ruprechtsplatz 1, tel: 533 53 32*. A trendy bar/restaurant in Hermann Czech's minimalist decor, it's frequented by writers, artists and night-owls. Sophisticated *nouveau* treatment of old imperial delicacies. Dinner, daily 5pm–12.30am, bar till 4am.

Stadtbeisl €€ *1, Naglergasse 21, tel: 533 35 07*. The old-fashioned interior with dark wood panelling is a fabled reminder of the old days. Reasonably priced Viennese dishes include *schnitzel*, goulash and dumplings. *Schanigarten*. Daily 10am–midnight.

Stomach €€ *9, Seegasse 26, tel: 310 20 99*. Austrian food with Styrian accent: lovely *Tafelspitz*, and vension, wild boar and trout in season. Popular, so reservation is required. Wed–Fri 4pm–midnight, Sat 10am–10pm.

Steirereck €€€ *3, Rasumofskygasse 2, tel: 713 31 68; <www. steirereck.at>*. A top-notch restaurant serving Austrian dishes, great wines and a grand selection of cheeses. Mon–Fri, *Wiener Gabelfrühstück* (elevenses) 10.30am–2pm, dinner 7pm–11pm.

Vorstadt € *16, Herbststrasse 37, tel: 493 17 88, fax: 495 29 32 4; <www.vorstadt.at>.* Once a typical *Beisl* in working-class Ottakring, it's been given a new lease of life by an enthusiastic young team, who offer traditional Viennese food and a varied programme of modern music and culture. Mon–Sat 11am–2am (hot meals till midnight).

Wrenkh €€ *1, Bauernmarkt 10, tel: 533 15 26.* A prize-winning restaurant, which is justifiably renowned for its vegetarian and wholefood dishes, cooked with Mediterranean/Asian influences. The bar is stylish and popular. Daily 11.30am–midnight; closed public holidays.

Zu den Drei Husaren €€ *1, Weihburggasse 4; tel: 512 10 92.* Elegant but comfortable restaurant serving beautifully prepared Viennese cuisine with romantic piano accompaniment. The place to go for an evening of gracious living. Interesting and varied selection of starters. Daily noon–3pm, 6pm–2.30am.

Zur Goldenen Glocke €€ *5, Kettenbrückengasse/Schönbrunner-strasse 8; tel: 587 57 67.* Serves good Viennese cuisine at moderate prices, using fresh produce from the nearby Naschmarkt. Popular for its garden. Mon–Sat 11am–2.30pm, dinner 5.30pm–midnight.

HEURIGER (WINE GARDENS)

Hengl–Haselbrunner €€€ *19, Iglaseegasse 10, tel: 320 33 30; <www.hengl-haselbrunner.at>.* A buffet to enjoy in a relaxed atmosphere, accompanied by some of the city's finest red wines. Viennese specialities include noodles with diced ham and curd-cheese dumplings; there are vegetarian dishes, too. 3.30pm–midnight.

Muth €€ *19, Probusgasse 10, Heiligenstadt, tel: 370 22 47.* A large attractive garden with old trees. Muth provides prize-winning wines, an enticing buffet and homemade fruit *strudel*. Children's playground. Mid-Jan–mid-Dec Wed–Mon 3.30pm–midnight.

Sirbu €€ *19, Kahlenbergerstrasse 210, tel: 320 59 28.* A short walk up Nussberg with fine wines to entice you. From the garden, there's a picturesque view across the vineyards to the Danube. Apr–mid-Oct Mon–Sat 3pm–midnight.

Weinhof Reichl €€ *21, Stammersdorferstrasse 41, tel: 292 42 33.* Excellent family cuisine with plenty of cherry and apple *strudel* to accompany the wines. Music in the garden on Saturday. Apr–Oct, Tues–Sun 2pm–midnight; Nov–Mar, Thur–Sun 2pm–midnight.

Weingut Reinprecht €€€ *19, Cobenzlgasse 22, tel: 320 14 71; <www.grinzing.net>.* Housed in a 300-year-old former monastery, the fine wines, copious buffet meals and good Viennese music make this a great experience. Mar–Nov, daily 3.30pm–midnight.

Winzerhof Leopold €€ *21, Stammersdorferstrasse 18, tel/fax: 292 13 56.* A modern and friendly *heuriger*, offering fine wines and a seasonal buffet. Feb, Apr, June, Aug, Oct, Dec: daily 2–11pm.

Zahel €€ *23, Maurer Hauptplatz 9, tel: 889 13 18.* An up-and-coming place with fine wines, a splendid buffet and *à la carte* menu. Comfortable, homely atmosphere. It's open 18 days from the first Thursday of every month, Tues–Sun 3pm–midnight.

STADTHEURIGER

Augustinerkeller *Brunch €, dinner €€ 1, Augustinerstrasse 1, tel: 533 10 26; <www.augustinerkeller.at>.* Close to the Albertina, this is an all-inclusive restaurant with music. From 6pm there's a *heuriger* buffet with wine and beer. Daily 11am–midnight.

Esterhazykeller € *1, Haarhof 1/Nähe Naglergasse, tel: 533 34 82; <www.esterhazykeller.at>.* One of the oldest wine cellars in Vienna, in operation since the Turkish siege of 1683. Also serves specialist beers. Mon–Fri 11am–11pm, Sat–Sun 4pm–11pm.

Melker Stiftskeller €–€€ *1, Schottengasse 3, tel: 533 55 30; <www.members.aon.at/melkerstiftskeller>.* Cavernous vault in which the Melk monastery sells produce from its vineyards, and some excellent crisp knuckles of pork, too. Tues–Sat 5pm–midnight.

Zwölf-Apostel-Keller €–€€ *1, Sonnenfelsgasse 3, tel: 512 67 77.* Named after its 300-year-old clock crowned with figures of the apostles, this cellar is in deep 17th-century vaults. A limited menu, but the place is always crowded. The blackcurrant wine is delicious and very potent. Cold food only. 4.30pm–midnight, closed July.

CAFÉS

Aida *1, Stock–im–Eisen–Platz 2, tel: 512 29 77; <www.aida.at>.* Aida is a chain themed in shocking pink with 1950s' decor. The coffee is wonderful (some Viennese say it's the best) and the *patisseries* a dream. Mon–Fri 6.30am–8pm, Sat 7am–8pm, Sun 9am–8pm.

Alt Wien *1, Bäckerstrasse 9, tel: 512 52 22.* A café bordering on a *Beisl* with a deliberately decadent and dingy atmosphere. It offers a mouth-watering selection of snacks. Interesting literary clientele in the evenings. Sun–Thur 9.30am–2am, Fri–Sat 9.30am–4am.

Café Bistro Anna *1, Wallnerstrasse 1, tel: 533 01 63.* A nice little café, distinguished by its friendly staff. The food is Italian/Austrian and comes in generous helpings. The tables outside are a pleasant spot to flop after exploring the city centre. Mon–Sat 8am–midnight.

Café Drechsler *6, Linke Wienzeile 22, tel: 587 85 80.* This café has been providing hot beverages to the market traders across the road for years. Now the night-owls have lit upon it. The food is good and so are the prices: cabbage *strudel*, paprika crêpes, goulash, fried cheese; and ham and eggs on fresh rolls for breakfast. 3.30am–8pm.

Café Restaurant KunstHaus Wien *3, Weissbergerlände, tel: 712 04 97; <www.kunsthauswien.com>.* Hundertwasser's last creation has an undulating floor and waterfall. Hearty Austrian grub, with creamy potato soup and juicy sausages. 10am–11pm.

Café Central *1, Herrengasse 14 (Palais Ferstel), tel: 533 37 64 24 <www.ferstel.at>.* The haunt of artists and intellectuals from times past, including Leon Trotsky and Peter Altenberg. Pricey, but glamorous. Mon–Sat 8am–10pm, Sun 10am–6pm, holidays 10am–6pm.

Demel K.u.K Hofzuckerbäcker *1, Kohlmarkt 14, tel: 535 17 17; <www.demel.at>*. Candies, crowds and cakes since 1796. Demel was, by appointment, pastry chef to Franz Jospeh and Sissi. It serves the daintiest delicacies in town. Cheap it isn't. 10am–7pm.

Frauenhuber *1, Himmelpfortgasse 6, tel: 512 43 23*. One of Vienna's oldest cafés (1824) and one of the prettiest. It's said that Mozart performed here and Beethoven was a regular. Exceptional menu. Mon–Sat 8pm–midnight, Sun 10am–10pm.

Hawelka *1, Dorotheergasse 6; tel: 512 82 30; <www.hawelka. com>*. Has a special treat,, the *'Buchkin'*, a yeast bun filled with jam, made by Frau Hawelka after 10pm. Mon, Wed–Sat 8am–2am, Sun 4pm–2am.

Indian Pavilion *1, Naschmarkt Stand 74–75, tel: 587 85 61*. This is a stall in the market and offers good Indian cooking. Mon–Fri 10.30am–6.30pm, Sat 10.30am–5pm.

Krah Krah *1, Rabensteig 8, tel: 523 81 93; <www.krah–krah.at>*. Krah Krah is a big pub with many beers, a large restaurant, bar and garden. Food is bread with various toppings. Daily 11am–2am.

Landtmann *1, Karl-Lueger-Ring 4, tel: 24 10 00; <www.landt mann.at>*. Always the most prestigious of the Ringstrasse cafés, next door to the Burgtheater. 7.30am–midnight.

Le Monde *1, Dr Karl-Lueger-Ring 8, tel: 535 46 65 <www. lemonde.at>*. *Schnitzel*, Asian wok dishes and espresso coffee are all on offer at this popular spot. Mon–Fri 9–1am, Sat, Sun 11–1am.

Livingstone and **The Planter's Club** *1, Zelinkagasse 4, Livingstone, tel: 533 33 93 15, Planter's Club, tel: 533 33 93 15*. The food is Californian/Pacific rim and well-prepared; the style is colonial. Daily 5pm–4am.

MAK **Café** *1, Stubenring 5, tel: 714 01 21; <www.mak.at>*. An ace café designed by Hermann Czech. Good Viennese food and vegetarian dishes, too. Tues–Sun 10am–2am.

Meierei im Volksgarten *1, Volksgarten, tel: 533 21 05*. This is an 'in' place with a secluded garden where you can relax after exploring Ringstrasse and the Imperial Palace. Apr–26 Oct, 8am–10pm.

Mozart *1, Albertinaplatz 2, tel: 24 10 00; <www.café-wien.at>*. There's been a café here since 1794. In Biedermeier times, it was a meeting place for artists, and is still in the premier spot to combine coffee and culture. 8am–midnight.

Prückel *1, Stubenring 24, tel: 512 61 15*. Situated opposite the Museum of Fine Arts, this is a fine old Viennese café, with a 1950s interior, serving a full menu. 8.30am–10pm.

Schottenring *1, Schottenring 19, tel: 315 33 43; <www.cafe-schottenring.at>*. Founded in 1879, this café combines ancient and modern with live music, wonderful desserts and internet access. Mon–Fri 6.30am–11pm, Sat–Sun 8am–9pm.

Café Sperl *6, Gumpendorfer Strasse 11, tel: 586 41 58; <www.sperltorte.at>*. Popular with Franz Lehár, and the meeting place of the stars, Sperl still attracts theatre people and literary types. Billiards and card tables. Mon–Sat 7am–11pm, Sun 11am–8pm.

Spittelberg area Between Siebensterngasse and Burggasse is an area of cobbled streets lined with baroque and Biedermeier buildings. Many house cafés and restaurants. Craft market on Saturday.

Trzesniewski *1, Dorotheergasse 1, tel: 512 32 91; <www.trzesniewski.at>*. Vienna's most famous sandwich bar, where you can stand and munch and people-watch. Daily 8.30am–7.30pm.

Ubl *4, Pressgasse 26, tel: 587 64 37*. Old-fashioned establishment serving good *schnitzels* and other classic fare such as *Zwiebelrostbraten* and *Tafelspitz*. Daily noon–2.30pm, 6pm–midnight.

Zum Kapuziner *1, Neuer Markt 2, tel: 512 92 02*. Opposite the Imperial Burial Vault, this comfortable establishment offers specialities such as beef goulash and roast duck. 11am–midnight.

INDEX